Elementary Phonics

by Florence Akin & Sonja Glumich

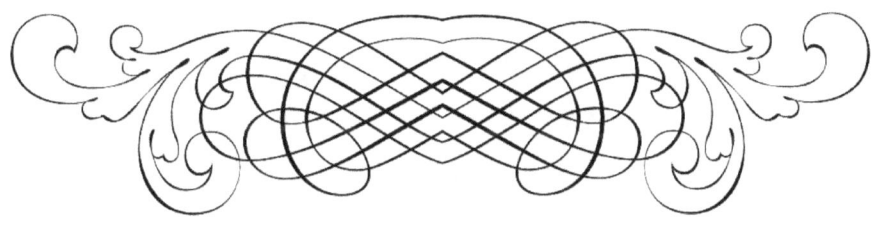

Phonics for Elementary School-Aged Children

A Three-Year Phonics and Vocabulary Building Program

Enlivens traditional phonics work with charming stories and poems, phonics games, and letter tile activities.

Under the Home Press Division
www.underthehome.org

Front Cover
ABC Letters
Image by Gerd Altmann
CC0 Creative Commons ({PD-US})
original source: *pixabay.com/en/letters-a-abc-alphabet-literacy-67046/*

Word Mastery, Original Copyright by Florence Akin, 1913
Published by Houghton Mifflin
The Riverside Press
Cambridge

Elementary Phonics, Copyright © 2018 Sonja Glumich
All rights reserved.

No part of this work may be reproduced, scanned, or electronically transmitted without prior permission of the copyright owner unless actions are expressly permitted by federal law the family exception detailed below.

The copyright owner grants an exception for photocopying or scanning and printing pages for use within an immediate family only. Scanned pages should never be used for any other purpose including sharing between families, posting online, transmitting electronically, or resale.

This exception does not extend to schools or co-ops, however a reasonable licensing fee for reproduction can be negotiated by contacting Under the Home, the publisher.

For more information, please contact Under the Home at contact@underthehome.org.

ISBN: 1948783037
ISBN-13: 978-1948783033

DEDICATION

For Chris, Everett, Cassidy, and Calista – my beloved family and curricula test squad.

TABLE OF CONTENTS

LESSON 1: PHONICS GAME (EAR TRAINING) 1

LESSON 2: GUESS THE WORD (EAR TRAINING) 2

LESSON 3: THE THREE LITTLE PIGS PART 1 (EAR TRAINING) 3

LESSON 4: PHONICS GAME (EAR TRAINING) 4

LESSON 5: GUESS THE WORD (EAR TRAINING) 5

LESSON 6: THE THREE LITTLE PIGS PART 2 (EAR TRAINING) 6

LESSON 7: PHONICS GAME (EAR TRAINING) 7

LESSON 8: GUESS THE WORD (EAR TRAINING) 8

LESSON 9: THE THREE LITTLE PIGS PART 3 (EAR TRAINING) 9

LESSON 10: GUESS THE WORD (EAR TRAINING) 10

LESSON 11: THE THREE LITTLE PIGS PART 4 (EAR TRAINING) 11

LESSON 12: GUESS THE WORD (EAR TRAINING) 12

LESSON 13: THE THREE LITTLE PIGS PART 5 (EAR TRAINING) 13

LESSON 14: PHONICS GAME (EAR TRAINING) 14

LESSON 15: GUESS THE WORD (EAR TRAINING) 15

LESSON 16: THE THREE LITTLE PIGS PART 6 (EAR TRAINING) 16

LESSON 17: PHONICS GAME (EAR TRAINING) 18

LESSON 18: GUESS THE WORD (EAR TRAINING) 19

LESSON 19: BLOW, WIND, BLOW! (EAR TRAINING) 20

LESSON 20: GUESS THE WORD (EAR TRAINING) 21

LESSON 21: A LITTLE SISTER (EAR TRAINING) 22

LESSON 22: PHONICS GAME (EAR TRAINING) 23

LESSON 23: FIRST SOUND AND LAST SOUND (TONGUE TRAINING) 24

LESSON 24: HOW MANY WORDS? LETTER "A" (TONGUE TRAINING) 24

LESSON 25: PRONOUNCE IT! (TONGUE TRAINING) 25

LESSON 26: HOW MANY WORDS? LETTER "B" (TONGUE TRAINING) 25

LESSON 27: PHONICS GAME (EAR TRAINING) 26

LESSON 28: FIRST SOUND AND LAST SOUND (TONGUE TRAINING) 27

LESSON 29: HOW MANY WORDS? LETTER "C" (TONGUE TRAINING) 27

LESSON 30: PRONOUNCE IT! (TONGUE TRAINING) 28

LESSON 31: HOW MANY WORDS? LETTER "D" (TONGUE TRAINING) 29

LESSON 32: PHONICS GAME (EAR TRAINING) 29

LESSON 33: FIRST SOUND AND LAST SOUND (TONGUE TRAINING) 30

LESSON 34: HOW MANY WORDS? LETTER "E" (TONGUE TRAINING) 30

LESSON 35: PRONOUNCE IT! (TONGUE TRAINING) 31

LESSON 36: HOW MANY WORDS? LETTER "F" (TONGUE TRAINING) 32

LESSON 37: PHONICS GAME (EAR TRAINING) 32

LESSON 38: FIRST SOUND AND LAST SOUND (TONGUE TRAINING) 33

LESSON 39: HOW MANY WORDS? LETTER "G" (TONGUE TRAINING) 33

LESSON 40: PRONOUNCE IT! (TONGUE TRAINING) 34

LESSON 41: HOW MANY WORDS? LETTER "H" (TONGUE TRAINING) 35

LESSON 42: PHONICS GAME (EAR TRAINING) 35

LESSON 43: FIRST SOUND AND LAST SOUND (TONGUE TRAINING) 36

LESSON 44: HOW MANY WORDS? LETTER "I" (TONGUE TRAINING) 36

LESSON 45: PRONOUNCE IT! (TONGUE TRAINING) 37

LESSON 46: HOW MANY WORDS? LETTER "J" (TONGUE TRAINING) 38

LESSON 47: PHONICS GAME (EAR TRAINING) 38

LESSON 48: HOW MANY WORDS? LETTER "K" (TONGUE TRAINING) 39

LESSON 49: GUESS THE WORD (EAR TRAINING) 39

LESSON 50: HOW MANY WORDS? LETTER "L" (TONGUE TRAINING) 40

LESSON 51: SOME LITTLE MICE (EAR TRAINING) 40

LESSON 52: HOW MANY WORDS? LETTER "M" (TONGUE TRAINING) 41

LESSON 53: PHONICS GAME (EAR TRAINING) 41

LESSON 54: GUESS THE WORD (EAR TRAINING) 42

LESSON 55: HOW MANY WORDS? LETTER "N" (TONGUE TRAINING) 42

LESSON 56: THE NORTH WIND (EAR TRAINING) 43

LESSON 57: HOW MANY WORDS? LETTER "O" (TONGUE TRAINING) 44

LESSON 58: PHONICS GAME (EAR TRAINING) 44

LESSON 59: FIRST SOUND AND LAST SOUND (TONGUE TRAINING) 45

LESSON 60: HOW MANY WORDS? LETTER "P" (TONGUE TRAINING) 45

LESSON 61: PRONOUNCE IT! (TONGUE TRAINING) 46

LESSON 62: HOW MANY WORDS? LETTER "Q" (TONGUE TRAINING) 47

LESSON 63: PHONICS GAME (EAR TRAINING) 47

LESSON 64: FIRST SOUND AND LAST SOUND (TONGUE TRAINING) 48

LESSON 65: HOW MANY WORDS? LETTER "R" (TONGUE TRAINING) 48

LESSON 66: PRONOUNCE IT! (TONGUE TRAINING) 49

LESSON 67: HOW MANY WORDS? LETTER "S" (TONGUE TRAINING) 50

LESSON 68: PHONICS GAME (EAR TRAINING) 50

LESSON 69: HOW MANY WORDS? LETTER "T" (TONGUE TRAINING) 51

LESSON 70: GUESS THE WORD (EAR TRAINING) 51

LESSON 71: HOW MANY WORDS? LETTER "U" (TONGUE TRAINING) 52

LESSON 72: WEE ROBIN'S CHRISTMAS SONG (EAR TRAINING) 52

LESSON 73: HOW MANY WORDS? LETTER "V" (TONGUE TRAINING) 53

LESSON 74: FIRST SOUND AND LAST SOUND (TONGUE TRAINING) 54

LESSON 75: HOW MANY WORDS? LETTER "W" (TONGUE TRAINING) 54

LESSON 76: PRONOUNCE IT! (TONGUE TRAINING) 55

LESSON 77: HOW MANY WORDS? LETTER "X" (TONGUE TRAINING) 56

LESSON 78: PHONICS GAME (EAR TRAINING) 56

LESSON 79: HOW MANY WORDS? LETTER "Y" (TONGUE TRAINING) 57

LESSON 80: GUESS THE WORD (EAR TRAINING) 57

LESSON 81: HOW MANY WORDS? LETTER "Z" (TONGUE TRAINING) 58

LESSON 82: THE CATERPILLAR (EAR TRAINING) 58

LESSON 83: THE SOUND OF M (EYE TRAINING) 59

LESSON 84: THE SOUND OF A (EYE TRAINING) 60

LESSON 85: THE SOUND OF N (EYE TRAINING) 61

LESSON 86: THE SOUND OF R (EYE TRAINING) 62

LESSON 87: THE SOUND OF F (EYE TRAINING) 63

LESSON 88: THE SOUND OF S (EYE TRAINING) 64

LESSON 89: THE SOUND OF E (EYE TRAINING) 65

LESSON 90: THE SOUND OF M, A, N, R, F, S, AND E REVIEW (EYE TRAINING) 66

LESSON 91: THE SOUND OF T (EYE TRAINING) 67

LESSON 92: THE SOUND OF L (EYE TRAINING) 68

LESSON 93: THE SOUND OF G (EYE TRAINING) 69

LESSON 94: THE SOUND OF C (EYE TRAINING) 70

LESSON 95: THE SOUND OF K (EYE TRAINING) 71

LESSON 96: THE SOUND OF B (EYE TRAINING) 72

LESSON 97: THE SOUND OF I (EYE TRAINING) 73

LESSON 98: THE SOUND OF H (EYE TRAINING) 74

LESSON 99: THE SOUND OF D (EYE TRAINING) 75

LESSON 100: THE SOUND OF P (EYE TRAINING) 76

LESSON 101: THE SOUND OF O (EYE TRAINING) 77

LESSON 102: THE SOUND OF J (EYE TRAINING) 78

LESSON 103: THE SOUND OF W (EYE TRAINING) 79

LESSON 104: THE SOUND OF U (EYE TRAINING) 80

LESSON 105: THE SOUND OF Z (EYE TRAINING) 81

LESSON 106: THE SOUND OF X (EYE TRAINING) 82

LESSON 107: THE SOUND OF Q (EYE TRAINING) 83

LESSON 108: THE SOUND OF V (EYE TRAINING) 84

LESSON 109: THE SOUND OF Y (EYE TRAINING) 85

LESSON 110: SHORT A – AT/AN (WORD BUILDING) 86

LESSON 111: SHORT E – ET/EN (WORD BUILDING) 87

LESSON 112: SHORT I – IT/IN (WORD BUILDING) 88

LESSON 113: SHORT O – OT/OP (WORD BUILDING) 89

LESSON 114: SHORT U – UT/UN/UP (WORD BUILDING) 90

LESSON 115: SHORT A – AP/AD (WORD BUILDING) 91

LESSON 116: SHORT E – ED/EM/EB/EX (WORD BUILDING) 92

LESSON 117: SHORT I – ID/IP (WORD BUILDING) 93

LESSON 118: SHORT O – OD/OG/OB/OX (WORD BUILDING) 94

LESSON 119: SHORT U – UG/UB/UD/UM (WORD BUILDING) 95

LESSON 120: SHORT A – AM/AB/AX (WORD BUILDING) 96

LESSON 121: SHORT I – IM/IB/IG/IX (WORD BUILDING) 97

LESSON 122: SHORT VOWELS – REVIEW 1 (WORD BUILDING) 98

LESSON 123: SHORT VOWELS – REVIEW 2 (WORD BUILDING) 99

LESSON 124: SHORT VOWELS – REVIEW 3 (WORD BUILDING) 100

LESSON 125: SHORT VOWELS – REVIEW 4 (WORD BUILDING) 101

LESSON 126: LONG A/I AND SILENT E (WORD BUILDING) 102

LESSON 127: LONG I/O/U AND SILENT E (WORD BUILDING) 103

LESSON 128: LONG A (WORD BUILDING) 104

LESSON 129: LONG I (WORD BUILDING) 105

LESSON 130: LONG O (WORD BUILDING) 106

LESSON 131: LONG U (WORD BUILDING) 107

LESSON 132: LONG E (WORD BUILDING) 108

LESSON 133: LONG VOWELS – REVIEW 1 (WORD BUILDING) 109

LESSON 134: LONG VOWELS – REVIEW 2 (WORD BUILDING) 110

LESSON 135: LONG VOWELS – REVIEW 3 (WORD BUILDING)	111
LESSON 136: PLURAL S FORM OF WORDS (WORD BUILDING)	112
LESSON 137: PLURAL S=Z FORM OF WORDS (WORD BUILDING)	113
LESSON 138: POSSESSIVE FORM OF WORDS (WORD BUILDING)	114
LESSON 139: COMBINATION – CK (WORD BUILDING)	115
LESSON 140: COMBINATION – LL (WORD BUILDING)	116
LESSON 141: COMBINATIONS – SS/FF/ZZ (WORD BUILDING)	117
LESSON 142: SHORT VOWEL FOLLOWED BY 2 CONSONANTS – PART 1 (WORD BUILDING)	118
LESSON 143: SHORT VOWEL FOLLOWED BY 2 CONSONANTS – PART 2 (WORD BUILDING)	119
LESSON 144: SHORT VOWEL FOLLOWED BY 2 CONSONANTS – PART 3 (WORD BUILDING)	120
LESSON 145: MISCELLANEOUS – REVIEW (WORD BUILDING)	121
LESSON 146: COMBINATION – CH (WORD BUILDING)	122
LESSON 147: COMBINATION – TCH=CH (WORD BUILDING)	123
LESSON 148: COMBINATION – SH PART 1 (WORD BUILDING)	124
LESSON 149: COMBINATION – SH PART 2 (WORD BUILDING)	125
LESSON 150: COMBINATION – VOICELESS TH (WORD BUILDING)	126
LESSON 151: COMBINATION – VOICED TH (WORD BUILDING)	127
LESSON 152: COMBINATION – WH (WORD BUILDING)	128
LESSON 153: MISCELLANEOUS – REVIEW (WORD BUILDING)	129
LESSON 154: COMBINATIONS – BL/CL/FL (WORD BUILDING)	130
LESSON 155: COMBINATIONS – SL/PL/GL (WORD BUILDING)	131
LESSON 156: COMBINATION – SP (WORD BUILDING)	132
LESSON 157: COMBINATIONS – BR/CR (WORD BUILDING)	133
LESSON 158: COMBINATIONS – SC/SK (WORD BUILDING)	134
LESSON 159: COMBINATIONS – DR/FR/SPR (WORD BUILDING)	135
LESSON 160: COMBINATIONS – GR/PR/TR (WORD BUILDING)	136
LESSON 161: COMBINATIONS – ST/STE (WORD BUILDING)	137
LESSON 162: COMBINATIONS – SM/SN/SW (WORD BUILDING)	138
LESSON 163: COMBINATIONS – TW/QU (WORD BUILDING)	139
LESSON 164: MISCELLANEOUS – REVIEW (WORD BUILDING)	140
LESSON 165: THREE SOUNDS OF Y – PART 1 (WORD BUILDING)	141
LESSON 166: THREE SOUNDS OF Y – PART 2 (WORD BUILDING)	142
LESSON 167: THREE SOUNDS OF Y – PART 3 (WORD BUILDING)	143
LESSON 168: COMBINATION – AI=LONG A (WORD BUILDING)	144

LESSON 169: COMBINATION – AY=LONG A (WORD BUILDING) 145

LESSON 170: COMBINATION – EA=LONG E PART 1 (WORD BUILDING) 146

LESSON 171: COMBINATION – EA=LONG E PART 2 (WORD BUILDING) 147

LESSON 172: COMBINATION – EE=LONG E PART 1 (WORD BUILDING) 148

LESSON 173: COMBINATION – EE=LONG E PART 2 (WORD BUILDING) 149

LESSON 174: COMBINATION – EE=LONG E PART 3 (WORD BUILDING) 150

LESSON 175: COMBINATION – IE=LONG I (WORD BUILDING) 151

LESSON 176: COMBINATION – OA=LONG O PART 1 (WORD BUILDING) 152

LESSON 177: COMBINATION – OA=LONG O PART 2 (WORD BUILDING) 153

LESSON 178: COMBINATIONS – OE=LONG O AND UE=LONG U (WORD BUILDING) 154

LESSON 179: ADDITIONAL LONG I WORDS (WORD BUILDING) 155

LESSON 180: COMBINATION – IGH=LONG I (WORD BUILDING) 156

LESSON 181: ADDITIONAL LONG O WORDS (WORD BUILDING) 157

LESSON 182: COMBINATION – OW (WORD BUILDING) 158

LESSON 183: COMBINATION – OU=OW (WORD BUILDING) 159

LESSON 184: COMBINATION – OW=LONG O (WORD BUILDING) 160

LESSON 185: COMBINATION – OU=LONG O (WORD BUILDING) 161

LESSON 186: COMBINATIONS – ING/INGS (WORD BUILDING) 162

LESSON 187: COMBINATION – ING IN TWO-SYLLABLE WORDS (WORD BUILDING) 163

LESSON 188: COMBINATION – ER (WORD BUILDING) 164

LESSON 189: COMBINATION – ERS (WORD BUILDING) 165

LESSON 190: MISCELLANEOUS – REVIEW 1 (WORD BUILDING) 166

LESSON 191: MISCELLANEOUS – REVIEW 2 (WORD BUILDING) 167

LESSON 192: MISCELLANEOUS – REVIEW 3 (WORD BUILDING) 168

LESSON 193: MISCELLANEOUS – REVIEW 4 (WORD BUILDING) 169

LESSON 194: COMBINATIONS – ANG/ONG/UNG/ENG (WORD BUILDING) 170

LESSON 195: COMBINATION – N=NG (WORD BUILDING) 171

LESSON 196: COMBINATION – ING AND DROPPING E PART 1 (WORD BUILDING) 172

LESSON 197: COMBINATION – ING AND DROPPING E PART 2 (WORD BUILDING) 173

LESSON 198: COMBINATIONS – KN=N AND GN=N (WORD BUILDING) 174

LESSON 199: COMBINATION – WR=R (WORD BUILDING) 175

LESSON 200: COMBINATION – MB=M (WORD BUILDING) 176

LESSON 201: COMBINATION – GU=G (WORD BUILDING) 177

LESSON 202: COMBINATION – BU=B (WORD BUILDING) 178

LESSON 203: COMBINATION – BT=T (WORD BUILDING) 179

LESSON 204: MISCELLANEOUS – REVIEW (WORD BUILDING) 180

LESSON 205: CONSONANTS AND VOWEL SOUNDS (WORD BUILDING) 181

LESSON 206: SAME SOUND DOUBLE CONSONANTS BETWEEN VOWELS (WORD BUILDING) 182

LESSON 207: TWO OR MORE CONSONANTS BETWEEN VOWELS (WORD BUILDING) 183

LESSON 208: ONE CONSONANT BETWEEN VOWELS (WORD BUILDING) 184

LESSON 209: COMBINATIONS – AI=SHORT I AND IE=LONG E (WORD BUILDING) 185

LESSON 210: COMBINATION – EA=LONG A (WORD BUILDING) 186

LESSON 211: COMBINATION – EA=SHORT E (WORD BUILDING) 187

LESSON 212: COMBINATION – ED (WORD BUILDING) 188

LESSON 213: COMBINATION – ED=D (WORD BUILDING) 189

LESSON 214: COMBINATION – ED=T (WORD BUILDING) 190

LESSON 215: MISCELLANEOUS – REVIEW (WORD BUILDING) 191

LESSON 216: COMBINATIONS – IE/EY=LONG E (WORD BUILDING) 192

LESSON 217: COMBINATIONS – EI/EIGH/EY=LONG A (WORD BUILDING) 193

LESSON 218: COMBINATION – LONG OO (WORD BUILDING) 194

LESSON 219: COMBINATION – O=LONG OO (WORD BUILDING) 195

LESSON 220: COMBINATION – U=LONG OO (WORD BUILDING) 196

LESSON 221: COMBINATION – OU=LONG OO (WORD BUILDING) 197

LESSON 222: COMBINATION – UI=LONG OO (WORD BUILDING) 198

LESSON 223: COMBINATION – EW=LONG OO (WORD BUILDING) 199

LESSON 224: COMBINATION – WH=H (WORD BUILDING) 200

LESSON 225: COMBINATION – EW=LONG U (WORD BUILDING) 201

LESSON 226: COMBINATION – OO=LONG O (WORD BUILDING) 202

LESSON 227: COMBINATION – SHORT OO (WORD BUILDING) 203

LESSON 228: COMBINATIONS – O/OUL=SHORT OO (WORD BUILDING) 204

LESSON 229: COMBINATION – U=SHORT OO (WORD BUILDING) 205

LESSON 230: COMBINATION – FUL (WORD BUILDING) 206

LESSON 231: COMBINATION – OY (WORD BUILDING) 207

LESSON 232: COMBINATION – OI=OY (WORD BUILDING) 208

LESSON 233: COMBINATION – LE PART 1 (WORD BUILDING) 209

LESSON 234: COMBINATION – LE PART 2 (WORD BUILDING) 210

LESSON 235: COMBINATION – TLE=LE (WORD BUILDING) 211

LESSON 236: C=S BEFORE E/I/Y (WORD BUILDING) 212

LESSON 237: G=J BEFORE E/I/J (WORD BUILDING) 213

LESSON 238: COMBINATION – DG=J (WORD BUILDING) 214

LESSON 239: COMBINATION – LY (WORD BUILDING) 215

LESSON 240: COMBINATION – LESS (WORD BUILDING) 216

LESSON 241: COMBINATION – NESS (WORD BUILDING) 217

LESSON 242: COMBINATION – EST (WORD BUILDING) 218

LESSON 243: COMBINATION – ER (WORD BUILDING) 219

LESSON 244: COMBINATION – AR=ER (WORD BUILDING) 220

LESSON 245: COMBINATION – EAR=ER (WORD BUILDING) 221

LESSON 246: COMBINATION – IR=ER (WORD BUILDING) 222

LESSON 247: COMBINATION – OR=ER (WORD BUILDING) 223

LESSON 248: COMBINATION – UR=ER (WORD BUILDING) 224

LESSON 249: COMBINATION – ISH (WORD BUILDING) 225

LESSON 250: MISCELLANEOUS – REVIEW (WORD BUILDING) 226

LESSON 251: COMBINATION – A LIKE ST(A)R PART 1 (WORD BUILDING) 227

LESSON 252: COMBINATION – A LIKE ST(A)R PART 2 (WORD BUILDING) 228

LESSON 253: COMBINATION – AU LIKE ST(A)R (WORD BUILDING) 229

LESSON 254: COMBINATIONS – LF=F AND LV=V (WORD BUILDING) 230

LESSON 255: COMBINATION – AIR (WORD BUILDING) 231

LESSON 256: COMBINATION – AR=AIR (WORD BUILDING) 232

LESSON 257: COMBINATION – EAR=AIR (WORD BUILDING) 233

LESSON 258: COMBINATION – ERE=AIR (WORD BUILDING) 234

LESSON 259: COMBINATION – EIR=AIR (WORD BUILDING) 235

LESSON 260: COMBINATION – AW (WORD BUILDING) 236

LESSON 261: COMBINATION – A=AW (WORD BUILDING) 237

LESSON 262: COMBINATION – AU=AW (WORD BUILDING) 238

LESSON 263: COMBINATION – AUGH=AW (WORD BUILDING) 239

LESSON 264: COMBINATION – OUGH=AW (WORD BUILDING) 240

LESSON 265: COMBINATION – OUGH=LONG O (WORD BUILDING) 241

LESSON 266: COMBINATION – A LIKE B(A)SKET (WORD BUILDING) 242

LESSON 267: COMBINATION – A=SHORT O (WORD BUILDING) 243

LESSON 268: COMBINATION – O=SHORT U PART 1 (WORD BUILDING) 244

LESSON 269: COMBINATION – O=SHORT U PART 2 (WORD BUILDING) 245

LESSON 270: COMBINATION – OU=SHORT U (WORD BUILDING) 246

LESSON 271: COMBINATION – OO=SHORT U (WORD BUILDING) 247

LESSON 272: OBSCURE A – PART 1 (WORD BUILDING) 248

LESSON 273: OBSCURE A – PART 2 (WORD BUILDING) 249

LESSON 274: OBSCURE A – PART 3 (WORD BUILDING) 250

LESSON 275: OBSCURE E (WORD BUILDING) 251

LESSON 276: OBSCURE O – PART 1 (WORD BUILDING) 252

LESSON 277: OBSCURE O – PART 2 (WORD BUILDING) 253

LESSON 278: OBSCURE U (WORD BUILDING) 254

LESSON 279: COMBINATION – EN=N (WORD BUILDING) 255

LESSON 280: COMBINATION – IN=N (WORD BUILDING) 256

LESSON 281: COMBINATION – ON=N (WORD BUILDING) 257

LESSON 282: COMBINATION – TEN=N (WORD BUILDING) 258

LESSON 283: COMBINATION – EL=L (WORD BUILDING) 259

LESSON 284: COMBINATION – EX=EGZ (WORD BUILDING) 260

LESSON 285: MISCELLANEOUS – REVIEW 1 (WORD BUILDING) 261

LESSON 286: MISCELLANEOUS – REVIEW 2 (WORD BUILDING) 262

LESSON 287: MISCELLANEOUS – REVIEW 3 (WORD BUILDING) 263

LESSON 288: MISCELLANEOUS – REVIEW 4 (WORD BUILDING) 264

LESSON 289: MISCELLANEOUS – REVIEW 5 (WORD BUILDING) 265

LESSON 290: COMBINATION – PH=F (WORD BUILDING) 266

LESSON 291: COMBINATION – GH=F (WORD BUILDING) 267

LESSON 292: COMBINATION – MN=M (WORD BUILDING) 268

LESSON 293: COMBINATION – CH=K (WORD BUILDING) 269

LESSON 294: COMBINATION – CH=SH (WORD BUILDING) 270

LESSON 295: COMBINATION – SC=S (WORD BUILDING) 271

LESSON 296: COMBINATION – I=Y (WORD BUILDING) 272

LESSON 297: COMBINATION – I=LONG E (WORD BUILDING) 273

LESSON 298: COMBINATION – QU=K (WORD BUILDING) 274

LESSON 299: COMBINATION – DI=J (WORD BUILDING) 275

LESSON 300: COMBINATION – TI=CH (WORD BUILDING) 276

LESSON 301: COMBINATION – SILENT H (WORD BUILDING) 277

LESSON 302: COMBINATION – ET=LONG A (WORD BUILDING) 278

LESSON 303: COMBINATIONS – CE/SI=SH (WORD BUILDING) 279

LESSON 304: COMBINATION – CI=SH (WORD BUILDING) 280

LESSON 305: COMBINATION – TI=SH (WORD BUILDING) 281

LESSON 306: MISCELLANEOUS – REVIEW 1 (WORD BUILDING) 282

LESSON 307: MISCELLANEOUS – REVIEW 2 (WORD BUILDING) 283

LESSON 308: MISCELLANEOUS – REVIEW 3 (WORD BUILDING) 284

LESSON 309: MISCELLANEOUS – REVIEW 4 (WORD BUILDING) 285

REFERENCES AND ADDITIONAL READING 286

What is Phonics?

Phonics, associating sounds with letters and blending those sounds into words, provides children with a foundation to decipher novel words.

About This Book

Make learning phonics entertaining and exciting with jump-out-of-your-seat phonics games, charming stories, and hands-on word building activities. This three-year phonics, vocabulary, and spelling program greatly expands upon Florence Akin's Word Mastery to accommodate instructors of all experience levels. Akin honed the leveraged instructional methodology in her own elementary classroom, incorporating four types of activities: 1) Ear Training, 2) Tongue Training, 3) Eye Training, and 4) Word Building.

The Targeted Audience for This Book Series

This series targets elementary school-aged children ages five and up.

How to Teach Using This Book

Cover as few or as many lessons as you wish per day. Progress upon lesson mastery by children. Ideally, hold two sessions of approximately 10 minutes each per day. At first indication of weariness or inattention, stop the lesson. The lessons are short, self-contained, and self-explanatory, such that no preparation is required on the part of the instructor, beyond obtaining letter tiles for later lessons.

Suggested Materials to Teach Using This Book

Letter tiles (A-Z and a-z with multiples of the common letters) are suggested for use with this textbook. You may either purchase the tiles or make them yourself out of heavy-duty paper or cardboard.

ELEMENTARY PHONICS

LESSON 1: PHONICS GAME (EAR TRAINING)

The instructor recites a series of sentences, pronouncing the lesson words in bold phonetically. In response, children stand to complete the actions and call out the words.

The instructor says:

- "Point at something **r-e-d**," enunciating the letter sounds of "red" very slowly (phonetically). *Children point at a red object and recite "red."*

- "Touch your **h-ea-d**."

- "**C-l-a-p** your hands."

- "Raise your **a-r-m-s**."

- "**J-u-m-p** on one foot."

- "**H-o-p** like a bunny."

- "Do five jumping **j-a-ck-s**."

LESSON 2: GUESS THE WORD (EAR TRAINING)

The instructor pronounces a series of words phonetically, drawing out each letter sound, and asks children to guess and call out each word.

P-i-g-s

M-a-n

N-o

I-n

P-i-g

ELEMENTARY PHONICS

LESSON 3: THE THREE LITTLE PIGS PART 1 (EAR TRAINING)

The instructor reads an excerpt from the story, "The Three Little Pigs." The instructor pronounces the dashed words phonetically and asks children to call out the words.

Once upon a time there were three little **p-i-g-s**.

One morning their mother said, "You must go out and make your living."

So they all set out.

The first little pig met a **m-a-n** with some straw.

He said, "Please give me some straw, I want to build a house."

The **m-a-n** gave the little pig some straw.

Then the little **p-i-g** made a house.

Soon an old wolf came along.

He knocked at the door and said, "Little pig, little pig, let me come **i-n**."

The little pig said, "**N-o**, no, by the hair of my chinny, chin, chin. I won't let you in."

The wolf said, "Then I'll huff and I'll puff, and I'll blow your house **i-n**."

So he huffed and he puffed, and he blew the house in.

Then he ate up the little **p-i-g**.

LESSON 4: PHONICS GAME (EAR TRAINING)

The instructor recites a series of sentences, pronouncing the lesson words in bold phonetically. In response, children stand to complete the actions and call out the words.

The instructor says:

- "Point at something **l-i-tt-le**," speaking the last word very slowly (phonetically). *Children point at a small object and recite "little."*

- "Pretend to pick up some **s-t-i-ck-s**."

- "Touch your **ch-i-n**."

- "Make a **h-u-ff**."

- "Walk like an **o-l-d** dog."

ELEMENTARY PHONICS

LESSON 5: GUESS THE WORD (EAR TRAINING)

The instructor pronounces a series of words phonetically, drawing out each letter sound, and asks children to guess and call out each word.

L-i-tt-le

S-t-i-ck-s

O-l-d

Ch-i-n

H-u-ff

LESSON 6: THE THREE LITTLE PIGS PART 2 (EAR TRAINING)

The instructor reads an excerpt from the story, "The Three Little Pigs." The instructor pronounces the dashed words phonetically and asks children to call out the words.

The second **l-i-tt-le** pig met a man with some **s-t-i-ck-s**.

He said, "Please give me some sticks, I want to build a house."

The man gave the little pig some **s-t-i-ck-s**, and he built a house.

Then the **o-l-d** wolf came along.

He knocked at the door and said, "Little pig, little pig, let me come in."

The little pig said, "No, no, by the hair of my chinny, **ch-i-n**, chin. I won't let you in."

The wolf said, "Then I'll **h-u-ff** and I'll puff, and I'll blow your house in.

So he huffed and he puffed, and he blew the house in.

Then he ate up the **l-i-tt-le** pig.

ELEMENTARY PHONICS

LESSON 7: PHONICS GAME (EAR TRAINING)

The instructor recites a series of sentences, pronouncing the lesson words in bold phonetically. In response, children stand to complete the actions and call out the words.

The instructor says:

- "Pretend to be a **w-o-l-f**," speaking the last word very slowly (phonetically). *Children pretend to be a wolf, perhaps growling and crawling, and recite "wolf."*

- "Make a **h-u-ff**."

- "Make a **p-u-ff**."

- "Pretend to build a wall of **b-r-i-ck-s**."

LESSON 8: GUESS THE WORD (EAR TRAINING)

The instructor pronounces a series of words phonetically, drawing out each letter sound, and asks children to guess and call out each word.

B-r-i-ck-s

W-o-l-f

P-u-ff

H-e

B-l-ow

LESSON 9: THE THREE LITTLE PIGS PART 3 (EAR TRAINING)

The instructor reads an excerpt from the story, "The Three Little Pigs." The instructor pronounces the dashed words phonetically and asks children to call out the words.

The third little pig met a man with some **b-r-i-ck-s**.

He said, "Please give me some bricks. I want to build a house."

The man gave the little pig some bricks, and he built a house.

Then the old **w-o-l-f** came along.

He knocked at the door and said, "Little pig, little pig, let me come in."

The little pig said, "No, no, by the hair of my chinny, chin, chin. I won't let you in."

"Then I'll huff and I'll **p-u-ff**, and I'll blow your house in," said the wolf.

"You may huff and you may puff, but you cannot blow my house in," said the little pig.

The wolf huffed and he puffed, and he huffed and **h-e** puffed.

But he could not **b-l-ow** the house in.

LESSON 10: GUESS THE WORD (EAR TRAINING)

The instructor pronounces a series of words phonetically, drawing out each letter sound, and asks children to guess and call out each word.

I-t

G-o

H-o-me

D-oo-r

P-o-t

LESSON 11: THE THREE LITTLE PIGS PART 4 (EAR TRAINING)

The instructor reads an excerpt from the story, "The Three Little Pigs." The instructor pronounces the dashed words phonetically and asks children to call out the words.

Then the wolf said, "Little pig, I know of a fine field of turnips."

"Where is **i-t**?" said the pig.

"Down in the field," said the wolf. "Will you **g-o** with me?

I will call for you in the morning. Then we can get some for dinner."

"I will be ready," said the pig. "What time shall we **g-o**?"

"At six o'clock," said the wolf.

The little pig got up at five o'clock, and he went to the field.

He got some turnips and ran **h-o-me**.

The wolf came at six o'clock.

He knocked at the **d-oo-r** and said, "Little pig, are you ready?"

"I went at five o'clock," said the pig, "and I have a **p-o-t** full of turnips."

LESSON 12: GUESS THE WORD (EAR TRAINING)

The instructor pronounces a series of words phonetically, drawing out each letter sound, and asks children to guess and call out each word.

T-r-ee

A-pp-l-es

H-o-me

L-e-t

G-a-r-d-e-n

R-a-n

ELEMENTARY PHONICS

LESSON 13: THE THREE LITTLE PIGS PART 5 (EAR TRAINING)

The instructor reads an excerpt from the story, "The Three Little Pigs." The instructor pronounces the dashed words phonetically and asks children to call out the words.

The wolf was angry, but he said, "Little pig, I know of a fine apple **t-r-ee**."

"Where is it?" said the pig.

"Down in the garden," said the wolf. "Will you go with me in the morning?

I will come at five o'clock. Then we can get some **a-pp-l-es**."

"I will go," said the pig.

This time the little pig got up at four o'clock.

He went to the **g-a-r-d-e-n**, and filled his bag with apples.

He was getting down, when he saw the wolf.

The wolf was very angry, but he said, "Little pig, are the apples good?"

"Very good," said the little pig. "**L-e-t** me throw you some."

The pig threw the **a-pp-l-es** far away.

The wolf **r-a-n** to get them.

Then the little pig ran home.

LESSON 14: PHONICS GAME (EAR TRAINING)

The instructor recites a series of sentences, pronouncing the lesson words in bold phonetically. In response, children stand to complete the actions and call out the words.

The instructor says:

- "Point **u-p**," speaking the last word very slowly (phonetically). *Children point upward and recite "up."*

- "Pretend to climb a steep **h-i-ll**."

- "Mime putting a **l-i-d** on a pot."

- "Pretend to ride on a merry-go-round horse at the **f-ai-r**."

- "Jump up **a-n-d** down."

ELEMENTARY PHONICS

LESSON 15: GUESS THE WORD (EAR TRAINING)

The instructor pronounces a series of words phonetically, drawing out each letter sound, and asks children to guess and call out each word.

F-ai-r

W-e

U-p

A-n-d

H-i-ll

L-i-d

LESSON 16: THE THREE LITTLE PIGS PART 6 (EAR TRAINING)

The instructor reads an excerpt from the story, "The Three Little Pigs." The instructor pronounces the dashed words phonetically and asks children to call out the words.

The next day the wolf came again and said, "Little pig, let us go to the **f-ai-r**."

"I will go in the morning," said the pig. "What time shall **w-e** go?"

"Let us go at three o'clock," said the wolf.

The next morning the pig got **u-p** at two o'clock.

He went to the fair **a-n-d** got a churn.

He was going home when he saw the wolf.

The little pig was frightened.

So he jumped into the churn to hide, and it rolled down the **h-i-ll**.

The wolf saw the churn rolling down the **h-i-ll**.

He was frightened, too, and ran home.

Next morning the wolf went to the little pig's house.

He said, "Little pig, I went to the fair. I met a great round thing on the way.

It was rolling down the hill. It frightened me, and I ran home."

"I frightened you," said the pig.

"I went to the fair at two o'clock, and I got a churn.

On the way home I saw you coming.

So I jumped into the churn, and it rolled down the **h-i-ll**."

The wolf was now very angry.

"I shall come down the chimney," he said, "and I shall eat you up."

The little pig made a fire. He hung a pot of water over it.

Soon he heard the wolf coming down the chimney.

He took the **l-i-d** off the pot. The wolf fell into it.

And the little pig had a good supper.

LESSON 17: PHONICS GAME (EAR TRAINING)

The instructor recites a series of sentences, pronouncing the lesson words in bold phonetically. In response, children stand to complete the actions and call out the words.

The instructor says:

- "**M-a-ke** a funny face," speaking the last word very slowly (phonetically). *Children make a funny face and recite "make."*

- "**G-o** to the left."

- "**B-l-ow** a kiss."

- "**G-o** to the right."

- "Pretend to eat some **c-o-r-n** on the cob."

- "Pretend to touch something **h-o-t**."

- "Puff like the **w-i-n-d**."

ELEMENTARY PHONICS

LESSON 18: GUESS THE WORD (EAR TRAINING)

The instructor pronounces a series of words phonetically, drawing out each letter sound, and asks children to guess and call out each word.

B-l-ow

W-i-n-d

G-o

M-i-ll

C-o-r-n

M-a-ke

H-o-t

LESSON 19: BLOW, WIND, BLOW! (EAR TRAINING)

The instructor reads the Mother Goose poem, "Blow, Wind, Blow." The instructor pronounces the dashed words phonetically and asks children to call out the words.

B-l-ow, **w-i-n-d**, blow!

and **g-o**, **m-i-ll**, go!

That the miller may grind his **c-o-r-n**:

That the baker may take it,

And into rolls **m-a-ke** it,

And send us some **h-o-t** in the morn.

ELEMENTARY PHONICS

LESSON 20: GUESS THE WORD (EAR TRAINING)

The instructor pronounces a series of words phonetically, drawing out each letter sound, and asks children to guess and call out each word.

C-a-ll

P-ee-p

W-a-t-er

D-ee-p

H-a-s

B-u-t

LESSON 21: A LITTLE SISTER (EAR TRAINING)

The instructor reads the Mother Goose poem, "A Little Sister." The instructor pronounces the dashed words phonetically and asks children to call out the words.

I have a little sister;

they **c-a-ll** her **P-ee-p**, Peep.

She wades in the **w-a-t-er**

d-ee-p, deep, deep;

She climbs the mountains,

high, high, high—

Poor little thing!

She **h-a-s b-u-t** one eye.

Note: The poem is a riddle, and the answer is a star.

ELEMENTARY PHONICS

LESSON 22: PHONICS GAME (EAR TRAINING)

The instructor recites a series of sentences, pronouncing the lesson words in bold phonetically. In response, children stand to complete the actions and call out the words.

The instructor says:

- "Pretend to put on a **h-a-t**," speaking the last word very slowly (phonetically). *Children mimic putting on a hat and recite "hat."*

- "Mew like a **c-a-t**."

- "Pant like a **d-o-g**."

- "Oink like a **p-i-g**."

LESSON 23: FIRST SOUND AND LAST SOUND (TONGUE TRAINING)

The instructor says a word and asks children to reproduce the first sound and the last sound. Start with the phonetic pronunciation of the word, and as children progress, advance to speaking the word normally.

H-a-t *The instructor asks children, "What is the first sound in h-a-t?" The instructor asks children, "What is the last sound in h-a-t?"*

C-a-p

C-a-t

D-o-g

P-i-g

LESSON 24: HOW MANY WORDS? LETTER "A" (TONGUE TRAINING)

The instructor challenges children to recite as many words as they can that begin with the sound of "A" as in "apple." The instructor writes the words on a whiteboard or sheet of paper as each is named.

ELEMENTARY PHONICS

LESSON 25: PRONOUNCE IT! (TONGUE TRAINING)

The instructor shows the following photos to children and asks them to pronounce each word phonetically.

H-a-t:

C-a-t:

D-o-g:

P-i-g:

LESSON 26: HOW MANY WORDS? LETTER "B" (TONGUE TRAINING)

The instructor challenges children to recite as many words as they can that begin with the sound of "B" as in "bird." The instructor writes the words on a whiteboard or sheet of paper as each is named.

LESSON 27: PHONICS GAME (EAR TRAINING)

The instructor recites a series of sentences, pronouncing the lesson words in bold phonetically. In response, children stand to complete the actions and call out the words.

The instructor says:

- "Pretend to write with a **p-e-n**," speaking the last word very slowly (phonetically). *Children pretend to hold and write with a pen and recite "pen."*

- "**F-a-n** your face with your hand."

- "Squeak like a **r-a-t**."

- "Pretend to cut down a tree to make a **l-o-g**."

LESSON 28: FIRST SOUND AND LAST SOUND (TONGUE TRAINING)

The instructor says a word and asks children to reproduce the first sound and the last sound. Start with the phonetic pronunciation of the word, and as children progress, advance to normally speaking the word.

P-e-n

F-a-n

R-a-t

M-a-n

L-o-g

LESSON 29: HOW MANY WORDS? LETTER "C" (TONGUE TRAINING)

The instructor challenges children to recite as many words as they can that begin with the sound of "C" as in "cat." The instructor writes the words on a whiteboard or sheet of paper as each is named.

LESSON 30: PRONOUNCE IT! (TONGUE TRAINING)

The instructor shows the following photos to children and asks them to pronounce each word phonetically.

P-e-n:

F-a-n:

R-a-t-s:

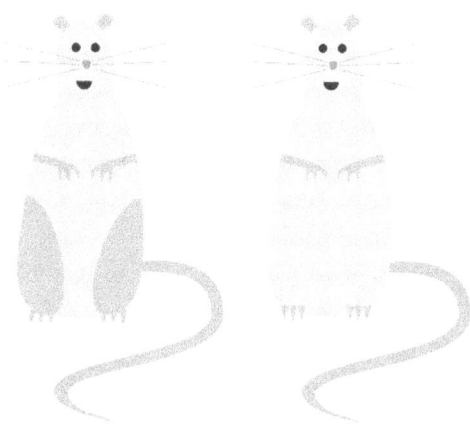

M-a-n:

L-o-g:

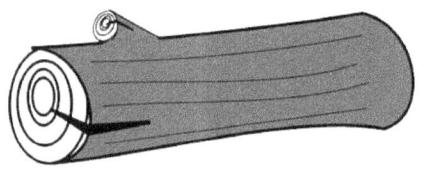

LESSON 31: HOW MANY WORDS? LETTER "D" (TONGUE TRAINING)

The instructor challenges children to recite as many words as they can that begin with the sound of "D" as in "dog." The instructor writes the words on a whiteboard or sheet of paper as each is named.

LESSON 32: PHONICS GAME (EAR TRAINING)

The instructor recites a series of sentences, pronouncing the lesson words in bold phonetically. In response, children stand to complete the actions and call out the words.

The instructor says:

- "Hop like a **f-r-o-g**," speaking the last word very slowly (phonetically). *Children crouch, hop like a frog, and recite "frog."*

- "Pretend to turn on a **l-a-m-p**."

- "Mime opening a **b-o-x**."

- "Cluck and peck like a **h-e-n**."

- "Pretend to sit on some eggs in a **n-e-s-t**."

LESSON 33: FIRST SOUND AND LAST SOUND (TONGUE TRAINING)

The instructor says a word and asks children to reproduce the first sound and the last sound. Start with the phonetic pronunciation of the word, and as children progress, advance to normally speaking the word.

F-r-o-g

L-a-m-p

B-o-x

H-e-n

N-e-s-t

LESSON 34: HOW MANY WORDS? LETTER "E" (TONGUE TRAINING)

 The instructor challenges children to recite as many words as they can that begin with the sound of "E" as in "elephant." The instructor writes the words on a whiteboard or sheet of paper as each is named.

ELEMENTARY PHONICS

LESSON 35: PRONOUNCE IT! (TONGUE TRAINING)

The instructor shows the following photos to children and asks them to pronounce each word phonetically.

F-r-o-g:

L-a-m-p:

B-o-x:

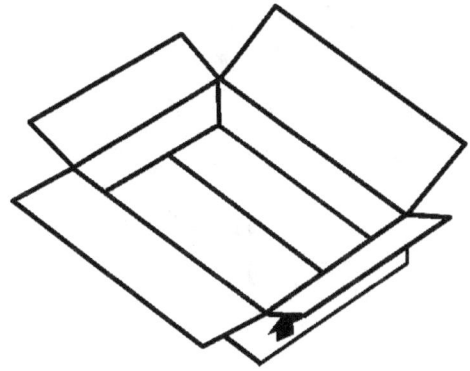

H-e-n:

N-e-s-t:

LESSON 36: HOW MANY WORDS? LETTER "F" (TONGUE TRAINING)

The instructor challenges children to recite as many words as they can that begin with the sound of "F" as in "fan." The instructor writes the words on a whiteboard or sheet of paper as each is named.

LESSON 37: PHONICS GAME (EAR TRAINING)

The instructor recites a series of sentences, pronouncing the lesson words in bold phonetically. In response, children stand to complete the actions and call out the words.

The instructor says:

- "Quack like a **d-u-ck**," speaking the last word very slowly (phonetically). *Children make a quacking sound like a duck and then recite "duck."*

- "Pretend to glide like a **s-w-a-n**."

- "Tweet like a **b-i-r-d**."

- "Crawl like an **a-n-t**."

LESSON 38: FIRST SOUND AND LAST SOUND (TONGUE TRAINING)

The instructor says a word and asks children to reproduce the first sound and the last sound. Start with the phonetic pronunciation of the word, and as children progress, advance to normally speaking the word.

F-o-x

D-u-ck

S-w-a-n

B-i-r-d

A-n-t

LESSON 39: HOW MANY WORDS? LETTER "G" (TONGUE TRAINING)

 The instructor challenges children to recite as many words as they can that begin with the sound of "G" as in "girl." The instructor writes the words on a whiteboard or sheet of paper as each is named.

LESSON 40: PRONOUNCE IT! (TONGUE TRAINING)

The instructor shows the following photos to children and asks them to pronounce each word phonetically.

F-o-x:

D-u-ck:

S-w-a-n:

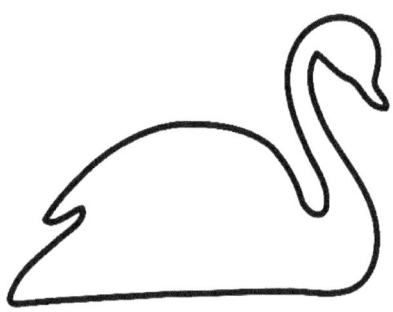

B-i-r-d:

A-n-t:

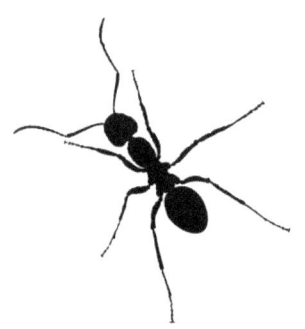

LESSON 41: HOW MANY WORDS? LETTER "H" (TONGUE TRAINING)

The instructor challenges children to recite as many words as they can that begin with the sound of "H" as in "hat." The instructor writes the words on a whiteboard or sheet of paper as each is named.

LESSON 42: PHONICS GAME (EAR TRAINING)

The instructor recites a series of sentences, pronouncing the lesson words in bold phonetically. In response, children stand to complete the actions and call out the words.

The instructor says:

- "Buzz like a **b-ee**," speaking the last word very slowly (phonetically). *Children make a buzzing sound and recite "bee."*

- "Pretend to cook some eggs in a **p-a-n**."

- "Pretend to drive a **v-a-n**."

- "Roar like a **l-i-o-n**."

- "Wave one **h-a-n-d**."

LESSON 43: FIRST SOUND AND LAST SOUND (TONGUE TRAINING)

The instructor says a word and asks children to reproduce the first sound and the last sound. Start with the phonetic pronunciation of the word, and as children progress, advance to normally speaking the word.

B-ee

P-a-n

V-a-n

L-i-o-n

H-a-n-d

LESSON 44: HOW MANY WORDS? LETTER "I" (TONGUE TRAINING)

The instructor challenges children to recite as many words as they can that begin with the sound of "I" as in "igloo." The instructor writes the words on a whiteboard or sheet of paper as each is named.

ELEMENTARY PHONICS

LESSON 45: PRONOUNCE IT! (TONGUE TRAINING)

The instructor shows the following photos to children and asks them to pronounce each word phonetically.

B-ee:

P-a-n:

V-a-n:

L-i-o-n:

H-a-n-d:

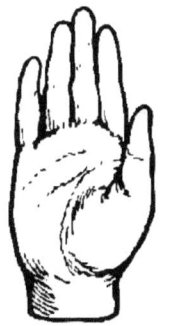

LESSON 46: HOW MANY WORDS? LETTER "J" (TONGUE TRAINING)

The instructor challenges children to recite as many words as they can that begin with the sound of "J" as in "jam." The instructor writes the words on a whiteboard or sheet of paper as each is named.

LESSON 47: PHONICS GAME (EAR TRAINING)

The instructor recites a series of sentences, pronouncing the lesson words in bold phonetically. In response, children stand to complete the actions and call out the words.

The instructor says:

- "**S-p-i-n** in a circle," speaking the last word very slowly (phonetically). *Children spin and recite "spin."*

- "Nod your **h-ea-d**."

- "Pretend to **c-u-t** a big piece of cake."

- "Shake your head **n-o**."

- "Pretend to **b-i-te** like a shark."

LESSON 48: HOW MANY WORDS? LETTER "K" (TONGUE TRAINING)

The instructor challenges children to recite as many words as they can that begin with the sound of "K" as in "kite." The instructor writes the words on a whiteboard or sheet of paper as each is named.

LESSON 49: GUESS THE WORD (EAR TRAINING)

The instructor pronounces a series of words phonetically, drawing out each letter sound, and asks children to guess and call out each word.

B-a-r-n

S-p-i-n

H-ea-d

C-u-t

N-o

B-i-te

LESSON 50: HOW MANY WORDS? LETTER "L" (TONGUE TRAINING)

The instructor challenges children to recite as many words as they can that begin with the sound of "L" as in "lion." The instructor writes the words on a whiteboard or sheet of paper as each is named.

LESSON 51: SOME LITTLE MICE (EAR TRAINING)

The instructor reads the Mother Goose poem, "Some Little Mice." The instructor pronounces the dashed words phonetically and asks children to call out the words.

Some little mice sat in a **b-a-r-n** to **s-p-i-n**,

Miss Puss came by, and put her **h-ea-d** in;

"Shall I come in and **c-u-t** your threads?"

"**N-o**, Miss Puss, you will **b-i-te** off our heads."

LESSON 52: HOW MANY WORDS? LETTER "M" (TONGUE TRAINING)

The instructor challenges children to recite as many words as they can that begin with the sound of "M" as in "moon." The instructor writes the words on a whiteboard or sheet of paper as each is named.

LESSON 53: PHONICS GAME (EAR TRAINING)

The instructor recites a series of sentences, pronouncing the lesson words in bold phonetically. In response, children stand to complete the actions and call out the words.

The instructor says:

- "Pretend to make a **s-n-ow** angel," speaking the last word very slowly (phonetically). *Children wave their arms and/or legs and recite "snow."*

- "Stamp your feet, **a-n-d** clap your hands."

- "Pretend to pull up a worm like a **r-o-b-i-n**."

- "Rub your hands together to keep them **w-a-r-m**."

LESSON 54: GUESS THE WORD (EAR TRAINING)

The instructor pronounces a series of words phonetically, drawing out each letter sound, and asks children to guess and call out each word.

B-l-ow

W-e

S-n-ow

A-n-d

R-o-b-i-n

W-a-r-m

H-i-s

LESSON 55: HOW MANY WORDS? LETTER "N" (TONGUE TRAINING)

The instructor challenges children to recite as many words as they can that begin with the sound of "N" as in "nest." The instructor writes the words on a whiteboard or sheet of paper as each is named.

LESSON 56: THE NORTH WIND (EAR TRAINING)

The instructor reads the Mother Goose poem, "The North Wind." The instructor pronounces the dashed words phonetically and asks children to call out the words.

The north wind doth **b-l-ow**,

And **w-e** shall have **s-n-ow**,

A-n-d what will the **r-o-b-i-n** do then,

poor thing?

He'll sit in a barn,

And keep himself **w-a-r-m**,

And hide **h-i-s** head under his wing,

poor thing!

LESSON 57: HOW MANY WORDS? LETTER "O" (TONGUE TRAINING)

The instructor challenges children to recite as many words as they can that begin with the sound of "O" as in "octopus." The instructor writes the words on a whiteboard or sheet of paper as each is named.

LESSON 58: PHONICS GAME (EAR TRAINING)

The instructor recites a series of sentences, pronouncing the lesson words in bold phonetically. In response, children stand to complete the actions and call out the words.

The instructor says:

- "Pretend to cradle a **d-o-ll**," speaking the last word very slowly (phonetically). *Children mimic holding a doll and recite "doll."*

- "Make a rumble like a **t-r-u-ck**."

- "Pretend to throw and catch a **b-a-ll**."

- "Pretend to tumble down a hill like **J-a-ck** and Jill."

LESSON 59: FIRST SOUND AND LAST SOUND (TONGUE TRAINING)

The instructor says a word and asks children to reproduce the first sound and the last sound. Start with the phonetic pronunciation of the word, and as children progress, advance to normally speaking the word.

D-o-ll

T-r-u-ck

T-oy

B-a-ll

J-a-ck

LESSON 60: HOW MANY WORDS? LETTER "P" (TONGUE TRAINING)

The instructor challenges children to recite as many words as they can that begin with the sound of "P" as in "parrot." The instructor writes the words on a whiteboard or sheet of paper as each is named.

LESSON 61: PRONOUNCE IT! (TONGUE TRAINING)

The instructor shows the following photos to children and asks them to pronounce each word phonetically.

D-o-ll:

T-r-u-ck:

T-oy:

B-a-ll:

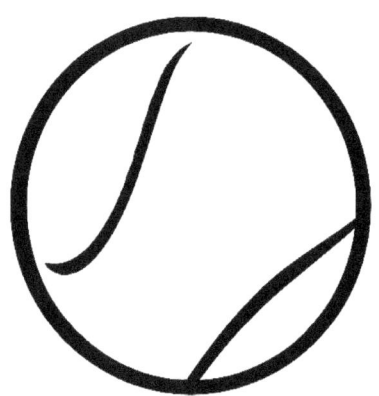

J-a-ck:

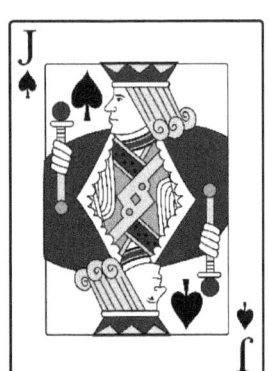

ELEMENTARY PHONICS

LESSON 62: HOW MANY WORDS? LETTER "Q" (TONGUE TRAINING)

The instructor challenges children to recite as many words as they can that begin with the sound of "Q" as in "queen." The instructor writes the words on a whiteboard or sheet of paper as each is named.

LESSON 63: PHONICS GAME (EAR TRAINING)

The instructor recites a series of sentences, pronouncing the lesson words in bold phonetically. In response, children stand to complete the actions and call out the words.

The instructor says:

- "Hoot like an **o-w-l**," speaking the last word very slowly (phonetically). *Children make a hooting sound and recite "owl."*

- "Pretend to eat a slice of **h-a-m**."

- "Flap your arms like a **b-a-t**."

- "Make a sound like a **c-a-r** horn."

- "Pretend to spread some **j-a-m** on toast."

LESSON 64: FIRST SOUND AND LAST SOUND (TONGUE TRAINING)

The instructor says a word and asks children to reproduce the first sound and the last sound. Start with the phonetic pronunciation of the word, and as children progress, advance to normally speaking the word.

O-w-l

H-a-m

B-a-t

C-a-r

I-n-k

J-a-m

LESSON 65: HOW MANY WORDS? LETTER "R" (TONGUE TRAINING)

The instructor challenges children to recite as many words as they can that begin with the sound of "R" as in "rabbit." The instructor writes the words on a whiteboard or sheet of paper as each is named.

ELEMENTARY PHONICS

LESSON 66: PRONOUNCE IT! (TONGUE TRAINING)

The instructor shows the following photos to children and asks them to pronounce each word phonetically.

O-w-l:

H-a-m:

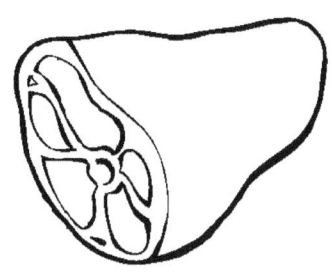

B-a-t:

C-a-r:

I-n-k:

J-a-m:

LESSON 67: HOW MANY WORDS? LETTER "S" (TONGUE TRAINING)

The instructor challenges children to recite as many words as they can that begin with the sound of "S" as in "snake." The instructor writes the words on a whiteboard or sheet of paper as each is named.

LESSON 68: PHONICS GAME (EAR TRAINING)

The instructor recites a series of sentences, pronouncing the lesson words in bold phonetically. In response, children stand to complete the actions and call out the words.

The instructor says:

- "**L-i-f-t** one foot," speaking the last word very slowly (phonetically). *Children raise one foot and recite "lift."*

- "**W-a-g** your finger."

- "**D-o** a little dance."

- "**C-l-a-s-p** your hands together."

- "**W-a-ve** your hands in the air."

LESSON 69: HOW MANY WORDS? LETTER "T" (TONGUE TRAINING)

 The instructor challenges children to recite as many words as they can that begin with the sound of "T" as in "tiger." The instructor writes the words on a whiteboard or sheet of paper as each is named.

LESSON 70: GUESS THE WORD (EAR TRAINING)

The instructor pronounces a series of words phonetically, drawing out each letter sound, and asks children to guess and call out each word.

R-o-b-i-n

B-u-sh

B-y

G-r-ay

S-o

C-a-n

W-i-fe

LESSON 71: HOW MANY WORDS? LETTER "U" (TONGUE TRAINING)

The instructor challenges children to recite as many words as they can that begin with the sound of "U" as in "umbrella." The instructor writes the words on a whiteboard or sheet of paper as each is named.

LESSON 72: WEE ROBIN'S CHRISTMAS SONG (EAR TRAINING)

The instructor reads the Mother Goose poem, "Wee Robin's Christmas Song." The instructor pronounces the dashed words phonetically and asks children to call out the words.

Wee **R-o-b-i-n** Redbreast hopped upon a **b-u-sh.**

An old gray kitty came **b-y** and said, "Where are you going, Wee Robin?"

Wee Robin said, "I'm going to the king. I shall sing him a song this good Christmas morning."

G-r-ay Kitty said, "Come here, Wee Robin, I will show you a bonny ring round my neck."

But Wee Robin said, "No, no, Gray Kitty. No, no, you worried the wee mouse, but you cannot worry me."

S-o Wee Robin flew away.

(continued next page)

Then Wee Robin came to the king's castle.

There he saw the king and queen.

"Now I shall sing my Christmas song," said Wee **R-o-b-i-n**.

So Wee Robin sang his good Christmas song.

Then the king said, "What **c-a-n** we give Wee Robin for his bonny Christmas song?"

"We can give him Jenny Wren for a **w-i-fe**," said the queen.

So Wee Robin and Jenny Wren flew away home.

LESSON 73: HOW MANY WORDS? LETTER "V" (TONGUE TRAINING)

The instructor challenges children to recite as many words as they can that begin with the sound of "V" as in "van." The instructor writes the words on a whiteboard or sheet of paper as each is named.

LESSON 74: FIRST SOUND AND LAST SOUND (TONGUE TRAINING)

The instructor says a word and asks children to reproduce the first sound and the last sound. Start with the phonetic pronunciation of the word, and as children progress, advance to normally speaking the word.

B-a-g

S-u-n

B-u-n-s

G-i-r-l

B-oy

LESSON 75: HOW MANY WORDS? LETTER "W" (TONGUE TRAINING)

The instructor challenges children to recite as many words as they can that begin with the sound of "W" as in "water." The instructor writes the words on a whiteboard or sheet of paper as each is named.

ELEMENTARY PHONICS

LESSON 76: PRONOUNCE IT! (TONGUE TRAINING)

The instructor shows the following photos to children and asks them to pronounce each word phonetically.

B-a-g:

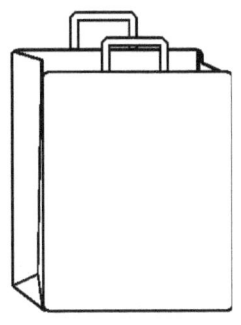

S-u-n:

B-u-n-s:

G-i-r-l:

B-oy:

LESSON 77: HOW MANY WORDS? LETTER "X" (TONGUE TRAINING)

The instructor challenges children to recite as many words as they can that include the sound of "X" as in "ax." The instructor writes the words on a whiteboard or sheet of paper as each is named.

LESSON 78: PHONICS GAME (EAR TRAINING)

The instructor recites a series of sentences, pronouncing the lesson words in bold phonetically. In response, children stand to complete the actions and call out the words.

The instructor says:

- "Do a **j-i-g**," speaking the last word very slowly (phonetically). *Children dance a jig and recite "jig."*

- "**S-w-i-m** with your arms."

- "**W-o-bb-le** your knees."

- "**P-oi-n-t** your toes."

- "Crawl like a **b-a-b-y**."

LESSON 79: HOW MANY WORDS? LETTER "Y" (TONGUE TRAINING)

The instructor challenges children to recite as many words as they can that begin with the sound of "Y" as in "yo-yo." The instructor writes the words on a whiteboard or sheet of paper as each is named.

LESSON 80: GUESS THE WORD (EAR TRAINING)

The instructor pronounces a series of words phonetically, drawing out each letter sound, and asks children to guess and call out each word.

F-u-rr-y

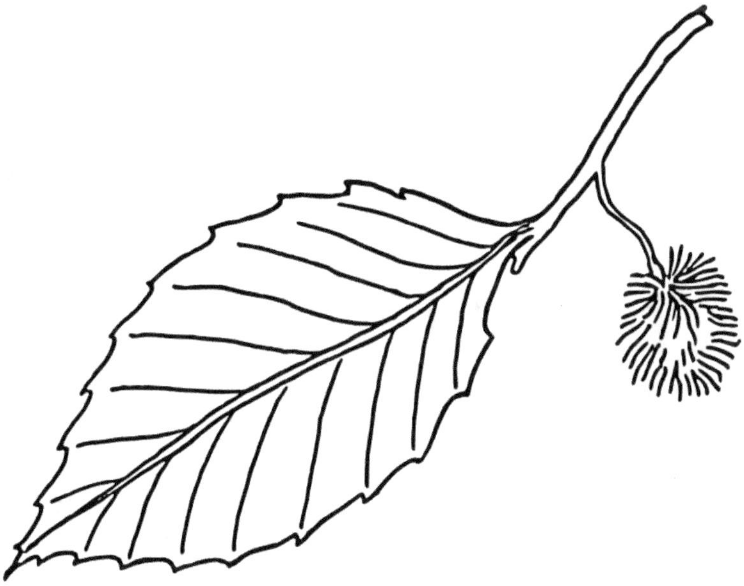

H-u-rr-y

L-ea-f

S-p-y

P-a-ss

S-p-i-n

T-o

LESSON 81: HOW MANY WORDS? LETTER "Z" (TONGUE TRAINING)

 The instructor challenges children to recite as many words as they can that begin with the sound of "Z" as in "zebra." The instructor writes the words on a whiteboard or sheet of paper as each is named.

LESSON 82: THE CATERPILLAR (EAR TRAINING)

The instructor reads the Mother Goose poem, "The Caterpillar." The instructor pronounces the dashed words phonetically and asks children to call out the words.

Brown and **f-u-rr-y**

Caterpillar in a **h-u-rr-y**;

Take your walk

To the shady **l-ea-f**, or stalk.

May no toad **s-p-y** you,

May the little birds **p-a-ss** by you;

S-p-i-n and die,

T-o live again a butterfly.

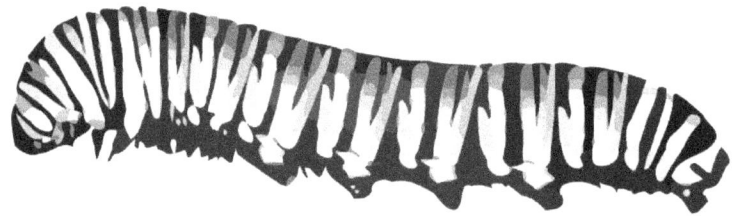

ELEMENTARY PHONICS

LESSON 83: THE SOUND OF M (EYE TRAINING)

Letter tiles (A-Z and/or a-z with multiples of the common letters) are suggested for use in many of the following lessons. You may either purchase inexpensive letter tiles or make them yourself out of heavy duty paper or cardboard.

The instructor:

- Asks children to name the pictures (*man* and *moon*).
- Asks children which sound comes first in *man* and *moon*.
- Tells children the letters (*M/m*) are pictures for the first sound.
- Points to the letters (*M/m*) and asks children to make the associated sound.
- Asks children to find the (*M/m*) tiles, to point at the tiles, and to make the associated sound.

LESSON 84: THE SOUND OF A (EYE TRAINING)

The instructor:

- Asks children to name the picture (*apple*).
- Asks children which sound comes first in *apple*.
- Tells children the letters (*A/a*) are pictures for the first sound.
- Points to the letters (*A/a*) and asks children to make the associated sound.
- Asks children to find the (*A/a*) tiles, to point at the tiles, and to make the associated sound.

ELEMENTARY PHONICS

LESSON 85: THE SOUND OF N (EYE TRAINING)

The instructor:

- Asks children to name the pictures (*nest* and *nut*).
- Asks children which sound comes first in *nest* and *nut*.
- Tells children the letters (N/*n*) are pictures for the first sound.
- Points to the letters (N/*n*) and asks children to make the associated sound.
- Asks children to find the (N/*n*) tiles, to point at the tiles, and to make the associated sound.
- Points at *man* and asks children to sound out the word (e.g. *m---a---n*, *m-a-n*, *man*).
- Asks children to build *man* out of tiles and to point at each tile while making the associated sound.

LESSON 86: THE SOUND OF R (EYE TRAINING)

The instructor:

- Asks children to name the pictures (*rat* and *rose*).
- Asks children which sound comes first in *rat* and *rose*.
- Tells children the letters (*R/r*) are pictures for the first sound.
- Points to the letters (*R/r*) and asks children to make the associated sound.
- Asks children to find the (*R/r*) tiles, to point at the tiles, and to make the associated sound.
- Points at *ran* and asks children to sound out the word (e.g. *r---a---n*, *r-a-n*, *ran*).
- Asks children to build *ran* out of tiles and to point at each tile while making the associated sound.

ELEMENTARY PHONICS

LESSON 87: THE SOUND OF F (EYE TRAINING)

The instructor:

- Asks children to name the pictures (*fan*, *fork*, and *fish*).
- Asks children which sound comes first in *fan*, *fork*, and *fish*.
- Tells children the letters (*F/f*) are pictures for the first sound.
- Points to the letters (*F/f*) and asks children to make the associated sound.
- Asks children to find the (*F/f*) tiles, to point at the tiles, and to make the associated sound.
- Points at *fan* and asks children to sound out the word (e.g. *f---a---n, f-a-n, fan*).
- Asks children to build *fan* out of tiles and to point at each tile while making the associated sound.

LESSON 88: THE SOUND OF S (EYE TRAINING)

The instructor:

- Asks children to name the pictures (*saw* and *sun*).
- Asks children which sound comes first in *saw* and *sun*.
- Tells children the letters (*S/s*) are pictures for the first sound.
- Points to the letters (*S/s*) and asks children to make the associated sound.
- Asks children to find the (*S/s*) tiles, to point at the tiles, and to make the associated sound.
- Points at *Sam* and asks children to sound out the word (e.g. *S---a---m, S-a-m, Sam*).
- Asks children to build *Sam* out of tiles and to point at each tile while making the associated sound.

ELEMENTARY PHONICS

LESSON 89: THE SOUND OF E (EYE TRAINING)

The instructor:

- Asks children to name the pictures (*egg* and *engine*).
- Asks children which sound comes first in *egg* and *engine*.
- Tells children the letters (*E/e*) are pictures for the first sound.
- Points to the letters (*E/e*) and asks children to make the associated sound.
- Asks children to find the (*E/e*) tiles, to point at the tiles, and to make the associated sound.
- Points at *men* and asks children to sound out the word (e.g. *m---e---n, m-e-n, men*).
- Asks children to build *men* out of tiles and to point at each tile while making the associated sound.

men

LESSON 90: THE SOUND OF M, A, N, R, F, S, AND E REVIEW (EYE TRAINING)

The instructor:

- Shows each word and asks children to sound out the words (e.g. *m---a---n*, *m-a-n*, *man* and *f--a--n*, *f-a-n*, *fan*).
- Asks children to build the listed words out of tiles and to point at each tile while making the associated sound.
    1. man
    2. fan
    3. men
    4. Sam
    5. ran

LESSON 91: THE SOUND OF T (EYE TRAINING)

The instructor:

- Asks children to name the pictures (*table*, *top*, and *turkey*).
- Asks children which sound comes first in *table*, *top*, and *turkey*.
- Tells children the letters (*T/t*) are pictures for the first sound.
- Points to the letters (*T/t*) and asks children to make the associated sound.
- Asks children to find the (*T/t*) tiles, to point at the tiles, and to make the associated sound.
- Shows *ten* and asks children to sound out the word (e.g. *t---e---n, t-e-n, ten*).
- Asks children to build the listed words out of tiles and to point at each tile while making the associated sound: ten, tan, mat, met, Nat, net, set, sat, rat

LESSON 92: THE SOUND OF L (EYE TRAINING)

The instructor:

- Asks children to name the pictures (*leaf*, *lemon*, and *lamp*).
- Asks children which sound comes first in *leaf*, *lemon*, and *lamp*.
- Tells children the letters (*L/l*) are pictures for the first sound.
- Points to the letters (*L/l*) and asks children to make the associated sound.
- Asks children to find the (*L/l*) tiles, to point at the tiles, and to make the associated sound.
- Points at *let* and asks children to sound out the word (e.g. *l---e---t*, *l-e-t*, *let*).
- Asks children to build *let* out of tiles and to point at each tile while making the associated sound.

ELEMENTARY PHONICS

LESSON 93: THE SOUND OF G (EYE TRAINING)

The instructor:

- Asks children to name the pictures (*gate* and *goose*).
- Asks children which sound comes first in *gate* and *goose*.
- Tells children the letters (*G/g*) are pictures for the first sound.
- Points to the letters (*G/g*) and asks children to make the associated sound.
- Asks children to find the (*G/g*) tiles, to point at the tiles, and to make the associated sound.
- Shows *gas* and asks children to sound out the word (e.g. *G---a---s*, *g-a-s*, *gas*).
- Asks children to build the listed words out of tiles and to point at each tile while making the associated sound: gas, get, gag, rag, tag, sag

LESSON 94: THE SOUND OF C (EYE TRAINING)

The instructor:

- Asks children to name the pictures (*cup*, *cat*, and *cap*).
- Asks children which sound comes first in *cup*, *cat*, and *cap*.
- Tells children the letters (*C/c*) are pictures for the first sound.
- Points to the letters (*C/c*) and asks children to make the associated sound.
- Asks children to find the (*C/c*) tiles, to point at the tiles, and to make the associated sound.
- Shows *cat* and asks children to sound out the word (e.g. *c---a---t, c-a-t, cat*).
- Asks children to build the listed words out of tiles and to point at each tile while making the associated sound: cat, can

ELEMENTARY PHONICS

LESSON 95: THE SOUND OF K (EYE TRAINING)

The instructor:

- Asks children to name the pictures (*kite*, *kettle*, and *key*).
- Asks children which sound comes first in *kite*, *kettle*, and *key*.
- Tells children the letters (*K/k*) are pictures for the first sound.
- Points to the letters (*K/k*) and asks children to make the associated sound.
- Asks children to find the (*K/k*) tiles, to point at the tiles, and to make the associated sound.
- Points at *keg* and asks children to sound out the word (e.g. *k---e---g*, *k-e-g*, *keg*).
- Asks children to build *keg* out of tiles and to point at each tile while making the associated sound.

LESSON 96: THE SOUND OF B (EYE TRAINING)

The instructor:

- Asks children to name the pictures (*ball*, *bird*, and *bell*).
- Asks children which sound comes first in *ball*, *bird*, and *bell*.
- Tells children the letters (*B/b*) are pictures for the first sound.
- Points to the letters (*B/b*) and asks children to make the associated sound.
- Asks children to find the (*B/b*) tiles, to point at the tiles, and to make the associated sound.
- Shows *bat* and asks children to sound out the word (e.g. *b---a---t*, *b-a-t*, *bat*).
- Asks children to build the listed words out of tiles and to point at each tile while making the associated sound: bat, bag, beg, cab, tab, Ben

ELEMENTARY PHONICS

LESSON 97: THE SOUND OF I (EYE TRAINING)

The instructor:

- Asks children to name the pictures (*igloo* and *iguana*).
- Asks children which sound comes first in *igloo* and *iguana*.
- Tells children the letters (*I/i*) are pictures for the first sound.
- Points to the letters (*I/i*) and asks children to make the associated sound.
- Asks children to find the (*I/i*) tiles, to point at the tiles, and to make the associated sound.
- Shows *bit* and asks children to sound out the word (e.g. *b---i---t*, *b-i-t*, *bit*).
- Asks children to build the listed words out of tiles and to point at each tile while making the associated sound: in, it, bit, sit, hit, fit, kit, wit, tin, fin, fig, fib, rib, bib, big, rim

LESSON 98: THE SOUND OF H (EYE TRAINING)

The instructor:

- Asks children to name the pictures (*horse*, *hat*, and *hand*).
- Asks children which sound comes first in *horse*, *hat*, and *hand*.
- Tells children the letters (*H/h*) are pictures for the first sound.
- Points to the letters (*H/h*) and asks children to make the associated sound.
- Asks children to find the (*H/h*) tiles, to point at the tiles, and to make the associated sound.
- Shows *hit* and asks children to sound out the word (e.g. *h---i---t*, *h-i-t*, *hit*).
- Asks children to build the listed words out of tiles and to point at each tile while making the associated sound: hat, hit, hem, ham, him, hen

ELEMENTARY PHONICS

LESSON 99: THE SOUND OF D (EYE TRAINING)

The instructor:

- Asks children to name the pictures (*doll, dog,* and *door*).
- Asks children which sound comes first in *doll, dog,* and *door*.
- Tells children the letters (*D/d*) are pictures for the first sound.
- Points to the letters (*D/d*) and asks children to make the associated sound.
- Asks children to find the (*D/d*) tiles, to point at the tiles, and to make the associated sound.
- Shows *red* and asks children to sound out the word (e.g. *r---e---d, r-e-d, red*).
- Asks children to build the listed words out of tiles and to point at each tile while making the associated sound: red, hid, sad, led, mid, dip, rid, had, did, lid, bed, dig, lad, mad, den, fed, bad, dim

LESSON 100: THE SOUND OF P (EYE TRAINING)

The instructor:

- Asks children to name the pictures (*pig* and *pear*).
- Asks children which sound comes first in *pig* and *pear*.
- Tells children the letters (*P/p*) are pictures for the first sound.
- Points to the letters (*P/p*) and asks children to make the associated sound.
- Asks children to find the (*P/p*) tiles, to point at the tiles, and to make the associated sound.
- Shows *pan* and asks children to sound out the word (e.g. *p---a---n*, *p-a-n*, *pan*).
- Asks children to build the listed words out of tiles and to point at each tile while making the associated sound: pan, pin, pen, pet, pat, pit, pig, peg, tap, rap, sap, nap, map, lap, cap, tip, rip, sip, dip, hip

LESSON 101: THE SOUND OF O (EYE TRAINING)

The instructor:

- Asks children to name the pictures (*octopus* and *owl*).
- Asks children which sound comes first in *octopus* and *owl*.
- Tells children the letters (*O/o*) are pictures for the first sound.
- Points to the letters (*O/o*) and asks children to make the associated sound.
- Asks children to find the (*O/o*) tiles, to point at the tiles, and to make the associated sound.
- Shows *log* and asks children to sound out the word (e.g. *l---o---g, l-o-g, log*).
- Asks children to build the listed words out of tiles and to point at each tile while making the associated sound: on, off, odd, log, rod, got, fog, pot, cob, hop, rob, nod, lop, hot, sod, top, pod, lot, dot

LESSON 102: THE SOUND OF J (EYE TRAINING)

The instructor:

- Asks children to name the pictures (*jam* and *jet*).
- Asks children which sound comes first in *jam* and *jet*.
- Tells children the letters (*J/j*) are pictures for the first sound.
- Points to the letters (*J/j*) and asks children to make the associated sound.
- Asks children to find the (*J/j*) tiles, to point at the tiles, and to make the associated sound.
- Shows *jam* and asks children to sound out the word (e.g. *j---a---m*, *j-a-m*, *jam*).
- Asks children to build the listed words out of tiles and to point at each tile while making the associated sound: jam, jar, jug, jet, jut, jab, jog, jug, job, jig

ELEMENTARY PHONICS

LESSON 103: THE SOUND OF W (EYE TRAINING)

The instructor:

- Asks children to name the pictures (*wagon* and *watch*).
- Asks children which sound comes first in *wagon* and *watch*.
- Tells children the letters (*W/w*) are pictures for the first sound.
- Points to the letters (*W/w*) and asks children to make the associated sound.
- Asks children to find the (*W/w*) tiles, to point at the tiles, and to make the associated sound.
- Shows *win* and asks children to sound out the word (e.g. *w---i---n, w-i-n, win*).
- Asks children to build the listed words out of tiles and to point at each tile while making the associated sound: wag, wig, wit, wet, web, win

LESSON 104: THE SOUND OF U (EYE TRAINING)

The instructor:

- Asks children to name the picture (*umbrella*).
- Asks children which sound comes first in *umbrella*.
- Tells children the letters (*U/u*) are pictures for the first sound.
- Points to the letters (*U/u*) and asks children to make the associated sound.
- Asks children to find the (*U/u*) tiles, to point at the tiles, and to make the associated sound.
- Shows *fun* and asks children to sound out the word (e.g. *f---u---n, f-u-n, fun*).
- Asks children to build the listed words out of tiles and to point at each tile while making the associated sound: up, gum, pug, run, hum, bun, fun, tug, gun, bug, tub, sun, hub, cut, rub, hut, mud, bud, rug, sup, hug, cup, but, jug, pup, nut

LESSON 105: THE SOUND OF Z (EYE TRAINING)

The instructor:

- Asks children to name the pictures (*zebra* and *zero*).
- Asks children which sound comes first in *zebra* and *zero*.
- Tells children the letters (Z/z) are pictures for the first sound.
- Points to the letters (Z/z) and asks children to make the associated sound.
- Asks children to find the (Z/z) tiles, to point at the tiles, and to make the associated sound.
- Points at *zoo* and asks children to sound out the word (e.g. *z---oo, z-oo, zoo*).
- Asks children to build the listed words out of tiles and to point at each tile while making the associated sound: zoo, zip, zap, zig, zag

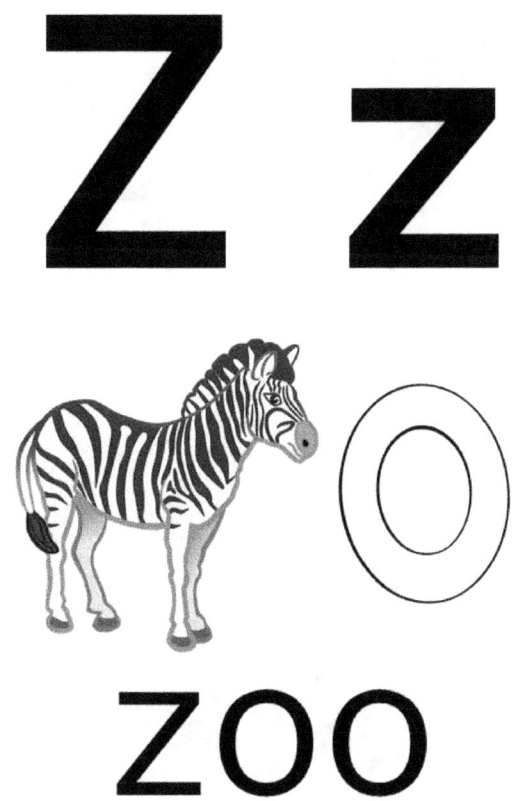

LESSON 106: THE SOUND OF X (EYE TRAINING)

The instructor:

- Asks children to name the pictures (*box* and *ax*).
- Asks children which sound comes last in *box* and *ax*.
- Tells children the letters (*X/x*) are pictures for the last sound.
- Points to the letters (*X/x*) and asks children to make the associated sound.
- Asks children to find the (*X/x*) tiles, to point at the tiles, and to make the associated sound.
- Shows *six* and asks children to sound out the word (e.g. *s---i---x*, *s-i-x*, *six*).
- Asks children to build the listed words out of tiles and to point at each tile while making the associated sound: ax, box, six, fax, fox

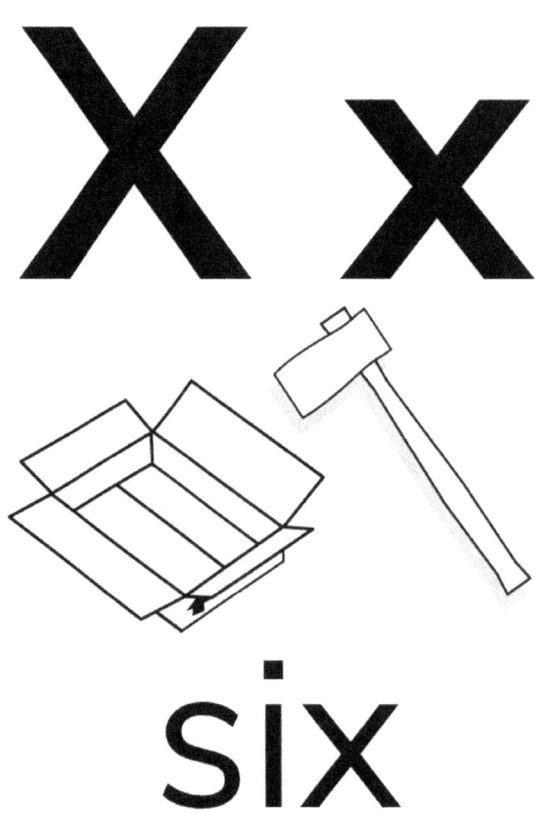

LESSON 107: THE SOUND OF Q (EYE TRAINING)

The instructor:

- Asks children to name the picture (*queen*).
- Asks children which sound comes first in *queen*.
- Notes that *Q* is typically paired with *u* in words.
- Tells children the letters (*Q/q*) are pictures for the first sound.
- Points to the letters (*Q/q*) and asks children to make the associated sound.
- Asks children to find the (*Qu/qu*) tiles, to point at the tiles, and to make the associated sound.

LESSON 108: THE SOUND OF V (EYE TRAINING)

The instructor:

- Asks children to name the pictures (*vine* and *vase*).
- Asks children which sound comes first in *vine* and *vase*.
- Tells children the letters (*V/v*) are pictures for the first sound.
- Points to the letters (*V/v*) and asks children to make the associated sound.
- Asks children to find the (*V/v*) tiles, to point at the tiles, and to make the associated sound.
- Shows *van* and asks children to sound out the word (e.g. *v---a---n*, *v-a-n*, *van*).
- Asks children to build the listed words out of tiles and to point at each tile while making the associated sound: vat, van, vet

ELEMENTARY PHONICS

LESSON 109: THE SOUND OF Y (EYE TRAINING)

The instructor:

- Asks children to name the picture (*yo-yo*).
- Asks children which sound comes first in *yo-yo*.
- Tells children the letters (*Y/y*) are pictures for the first sound.
- Points to the letters (*Y/y*) and asks children to make the associated sound.
- Asks children to find the (*Y/y*) tiles, to point at the tiles, and to make the associated sound.
- Shows *yet* and asks children to sound out the word (e.g. *y---e---t*, *y-e-t*, *yet*).
- Asks children to build the listed words out of tiles and to point at each tile while making the associated sound: yes, yet, yip, yak, yam, yap

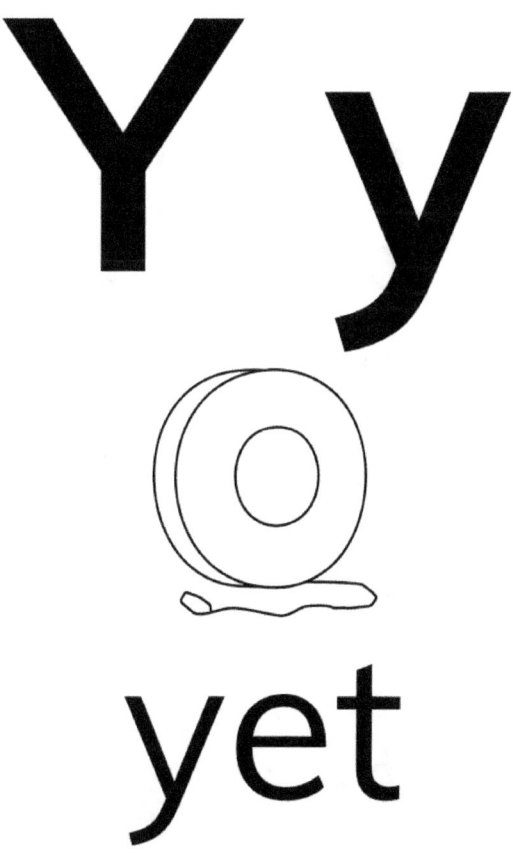

LESSON 110: SHORT A – AT/AN (WORD BUILDING)

The instructor demonstrates the *short a* sound and asks children to repeat the sound.

For each word, the instructor:

- Displays the word, asks children to sound out the word, and allows children to decipher the word with minimal assistance.
- Recites the word aloud and directs children to:
  1. Build the word out of letter tiles.
  2. Point at each letter tile in the word while making the related sound.

Note: For the remainder of the lessons in the book, mastery occurs when the instructor points to any word on a given list and children can sound it out on their own.

short a

at	an
c at	c an
b at	f an
h at	m an
s at	p an
m at	r an
p at	
r at	

ELEMENTARY PHONICS

LESSON 111: SHORT E – ET/EN (WORD BUILDING)

The instructor demonstrates the *short e* sound and asks children to repeat the sound.

For each word, the instructor:

- Displays the word, asks children to sound out the word, and allows children to decipher the word with minimal assistance.
- Recites the word aloud and directs children to:
    1. Build the word out of letter tiles.
    2. Point at each letter tile in the word while making the related sound.

short e

n et	h en
p et	m en
g et	p en
l et	t en
w et	B en
s et	d en
m et	

LESSON 112: SHORT I – IT/IN (WORD BUILDING)

The instructor demonstrates the *short i* sound and asks children to repeat the sound.

For each word, the instructor:

- Displays the word, asks children to sound out the word, and allows children to decipher the word with minimal assistance.
- Recites the word aloud and directs children to:
    1. Build the word out of letter tiles.
    2. Point at each letter tile in the word while making the related sound.

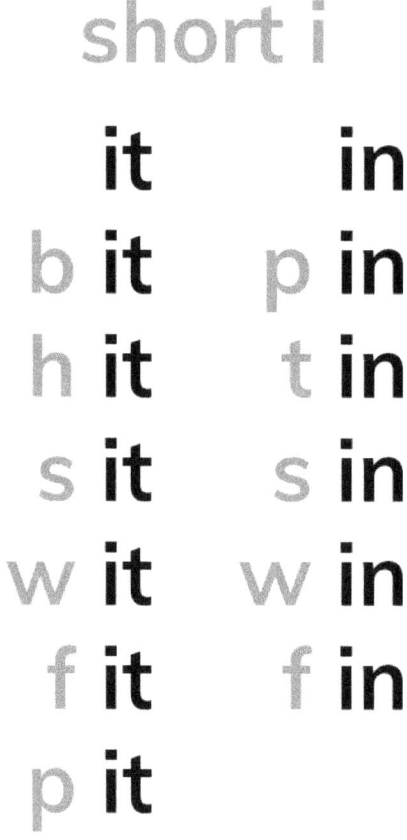

LESSON 113: SHORT O – OT/OP (WORD BUILDING)

The instructor demonstrates the *short o* sound and asks children to repeat the sound.

For each word, the instructor:

- Displays the word, asks children to sound out the word, and allows children to decipher the word with minimal assistance.
- Recites the word aloud and directs children to:
    1. Build the word out of letter tiles.
    2. Point at each letter tile in the word while making the related sound.

short o

d ot	h op
h ot	m op
l ot	p op
p ot	t op
c ot	l op
t ot	s op
n ot	
g ot	

LESSON 114: SHORT U – UT/UN/UP (WORD BUILDING)

The instructor demonstrates the *short u* sound and asks children to repeat the sound.

For each word, the instructor:

- Displays the word, asks children to sound out the word, and allows children to decipher the word with minimal assistance.
- Recites the word aloud and directs children to:
    1. Build the word out of letter tiles.
    2. Point at each letter tile in the word while making the related sound.

short u

c ut	s un	up
n ut	g un	c up
b ut	f un	p up
r ut	r un	s up
h ut	b un	

ELEMENTARY PHONICS

LESSON 115: SHORT A – AP/AD (WORD BUILDING)

The instructor demonstrates the *short a* sound and asks children to repeat the sound.

For each word, the instructor:

- Displays the word, asks children to sound out the word, and allows children to decipher the word with minimal assistance.
- Recites the word aloud and directs children to:
    1. Build the word out of letter tiles.
    2. Point at each letter tile in the word while making the related sound.

short a

c ap	b ad
l ap	h ad
m ap	m ad
n ap	s ad
g ap	p ad
s ap	l ad
t ap	
r ap	

LESSON 116: SHORT E – ED/EM/EB/EX (WORD BUILDING)

The instructor demonstrates the *short e* sound and asks children to repeat the sound.

For each word, the instructor:

- Displays the word, asks children to sound out the word, and allows children to decipher the word with minimal assistance.
- Recites the word aloud and directs children to:
  1. Build the word out of letter tiles.
  2. Point at each letter tile in the word while making the related sound.

short e

r ed   h em

l ed   w eb

f ed   R ex

b ed   v ex

N ed

LESSON 117: SHORT I – ID/IP (WORD BUILDING)

The instructor demonstrates the *short i* sound and asks children to repeat the sound.

For each word, the instructor:

- Displays the word, asks children to sound out the word, and allows children to decipher the word with minimal assistance.
- Recites the word aloud and directs children to:
    1. Build the word out of letter tiles.
    2. Point at each letter tile in the word while making the related sound.

short i

h id	d ip
d id	h ip
l id	l ip
m id	r ip
b id	t ip
k id	p ip
r id	s ip

LESSON 118: SHORT O – OD/OG/OB/OX (WORD BUILDING)

The instructor demonstrates the *short o* sound and asks children to repeat the sound.

For each word, the instructor:

- Displays the word, asks children to sound out the word, and allows children to decipher the word with minimal assistance.
- Recites the word aloud and directs children to:
    1. Build the word out of letter tiles.
    2. Point at each letter tile in the word while making the related sound.

short o

p od	h og	m ob	ox
r od	l og	r ob	b ox
n od	f og	c ob	f ox
s od		s ob	

ELEMENTARY PHONICS

LESSON 119: SHORT U – UG/UB/UD/UM (WORD BUILDING)

The instructor demonstrates the *short u* sound and asks children to repeat the sound.

For each word, the instructor:

- Displays the word, asks children to sound out the word, and allows children to decipher the word with minimal assistance.
- Recites the word aloud and directs children to:
    1. Build the word out of letter tiles.
    2. Point at each letter tile in the word while making the related sound.

short u

m ug	h ub
p ug	r ub
b ug	t ub
h ug	m ud
r ug	b ud
j ug	
t ug	g um
	h um

LESSON 120: SHORT A – AM/AB/AX (WORD BUILDING)

The instructor demonstrates the *short a* sound and asks children to repeat the sound.

For each word, the instructor:

- Displays the word, asks children to sound out the word, and allows children to decipher the word with minimal assistance.
- Recites the word aloud and directs children to:
    1. Build the word out of letter tiles.
    2. Point at each letter tile in the word while making the related sound.

LESSON 121: SHORT I – IM/IB/IG/IX (WORD BUILDING)

The instructor demonstrates the *short i* sound and asks children to repeat the sound.

For each word, the instructor:

- Displays the word, asks children to sound out the word, and allows children to decipher the word with minimal assistance.
- Recites the word aloud and directs children to:
    1. Build the word out of letter tiles.
    2. Point at each letter tile in the word while making the related sound.

short i

h im	w ig	m ix
d im	d ig	s ix
r im	p ig	f ix
b ib	b ig	
r ib	f ig	
	j ig	

LESSON 122: SHORT VOWELS – REVIEW 1 (WORD BUILDING)

The instructor demonstrates the *short vowel* sounds and asks children to repeat the sounds.

For each word, the instructor:

- Displays the word, asks children to sound out the word, and allows children to decipher the word with minimal assistance.

- Recites the word aloud and directs children to:
    1. Build the word out of letter tiles.
    2. Point at each letter tile in the word while making the related sound.

Review

an	b at	c ab	d en	f an	g as
at	b ad	c at	d ip	f at	g et
am	b ed	c an	d id	f ed	g ot
ax	b ig	c ap	d ig	f ig	g um
	b it	c ob	d im	f in	g ut
	b ox	c ot	d ot	f it	
	b ug	c ub	d in	f og	
		c up	d ug	f ox	
		c ut		f un	

ELEMENTARY PHONICS

LESSON 123: SHORT VOWELS – REVIEW 2 (WORD BUILDING)

The instructor demonstrates the *short vowel* sounds and asks children to repeat the sounds.

For each word, the instructor:

- Displays the word, asks children to sound out the word, and allows children to decipher the word with minimal assistance.
- Recites the word aloud and directs children to:
  1. Build the word out of letter tiles.
  2. Point at each letter tile in the word while making the related sound.

Review

h at	h ut	if	l ad	m an	n ap	on
h ad	h op	it	l ap	m ad	n et	ox
h am	h og	in	l et	m ap	n ot	p an
h en	h ot	j am	l ed	m at	n od	p at
h id	h ug	j et	l ip	m en	n ut	p en
h im	h um	j ug	l id	m et		
h ip	h ut		l og	m ix		
h it				m ud		

LESSON 124: SHORT VOWELS – REVIEW 3 (WORD BUILDING)

The instructor demonstrates the *short vowel* sounds and asks children to repeat the sounds.

For each word, the instructor:

- Displays the word, asks children to sound out the word, and allows children to decipher the word with minimal assistance.
- Recites the word aloud and directs children to:
    1. Build the word out of letter tiles.
    2. Point at each letter tile in the word while making the related sound.

Review

p et	r ed	s ad	t an	up	w ax
p ig	r im	s ap	t ap	us	w eb
p in	r ip	s et	t ax	v an	w et
p od	r ob	s in	t en	v at	w ig
p op	r ug	s it	t in	v ex	w in
p ug	r un	s ob	t ip	y es	z ig
		s od	t op	y et	
			t ub		
			t ug		

ELEMENTARY PHONICS

LESSON 125: SHORT VOWELS – REVIEW 4 (WORD BUILDING)

The instructor demonstrates the *short vowel* sounds and asks children to repeat the sounds.

For each word, the instructor:

- Displays the word, asks children to sound out the word, and allows children to decipher the word with minimal assistance.
- Recites the word aloud and directs children to:
    1. Build the word out of letter tiles.
    2. Point at each letter tile in the word while making the related sound.

Review

can	bed	Ben	rug	fig	cup
bit	fed	run	Nan	rob	tip
ham	sit	let	rap	vex	sad
let	did	pat	map	jug	wax
Dan	lid	Tom	bed	rib	mix
lip	led	ten	bat	top	tub
rod	cab	hem	red	box	bit
log	mat				

LESSON 126: LONG A/I AND SILENT E (WORD BUILDING)

The instructor:

- Tells children that unlike short vowels, long vowels are pronounced like the name of their letter. For example, *long a* is pronounced like the name of letter *A*.

- Asks children to repeat the following sounds:
    1. Short a (as in *at*)
    2. Long a (as in *ate*)
    3. Short i (as in *hid*)
    4. Long i (as in *hide*)

- Advises children that the *e* on the end of lesson words is silent and changes the preceding vowel from short to long.

- Displays each word, asks children to sound out each word, and allows children to decipher each word with minimal assistance.

- Recites each word aloud and directs children to:
    1. Build the word out of letter tiles.
    2. Point at each letter tile in the word while making the related sound.

long a/i and silent e

at	f at	c ap	S am
ate	f ate	c ape	s ame
h at	c an	t ap	d im
h ate	c ane	t ape	d ime
m at	p an	m ad	h id
m ate	p ane	m ade	h ide
r at	m an	f ad	
r ate	m ane	f ade	

ELEMENTARY PHONICS

LESSON 127: LONG I/O/U AND SILENT E (WORD BUILDING)

The instructor:

- Reminds children that long vowels are pronounced like the name of their letter.

- Asks children to repeat the following sounds:
    1. Short i (as in *pin*)
    2. Long i (as in *pine*)
    3. Short o (as in *rob*)
    4. Long o (as in *robe*)
    5. Short u (as in *tub*)
    6. Long u (as in *tube*)

- Advises children that the *e* on the end of lesson words is silent and changes the preceding vowel from short to long.

- Displays each word, asks children to sound out each word, and allows children to decipher each word with minimal assistance.

- Recites each word aloud and directs children to:
    1. Build the word out of letter tiles.
    2. Point at each letter tile in the word while making the related sound.

long i/o/u and silent e

f in	d in	r od	l op	t ub
f ine	d ine	r ode	l ope	t ube
p in	r ip	r ob	n ot	c ub
p ine	r ipe	r obe	n ote	c ube
t in	b it	h op	c ut	us
t ine	b ite	h ope	c ute	use
w in	r id	m op		
w ine	r ide	m ope		

LESSON 128: LONG A (WORD BUILDING)

The instructor:

- Reminds children that long vowels are pronounced like the name of their letter.
- Asks children to repeat the following sounds:
    1. Short a (as in *pal*)
    2. Long a (as in *pale*)
- Advises children that the *e* on the end of lesson words is silent and changes the preceding vowel from short to long.
- Displays each word, asks children to sound out each word, and allows children to decipher each word with minimal assistance.
- Recites each word aloud and directs children to:
    1. Build the word out of letter tiles.
    2. Point at each letter tile in the word while making the related sound.

long a

b ase	g ale	c ave	s ake
c ase	p ale	g ave	b ake
v ase	s ale	p ave	r ake
K ate	t ale	s ave	c ake
d ate	c ame	w ave	l ake
g ate	g ame	g aze	w ake
l ate	n ame	w ade	m ake
J ane	l ame		t ake
l ane	t ame		

LESSON 129: LONG I (WORD BUILDING)

The instructor:

- Reminds children that long vowels are pronounced like the name of their letter.

- Asks children to repeat the following sounds:
    1. Short i (as in *kit*)
    2. Long i (as in *kite*)

- Advises children that the *e* on the end of lesson words is silent and changes the preceding vowel from short to long.

- Displays each word, asks children to sound out each word, and allows children to decipher each word with minimal assistance.

- Recites each word aloud and directs children to:
    1. Build the word out of letter tiles.
    2. Point at each letter tile in the word while making the related sound.

long i

m ine	l ife	f ire
l ine	w ife	m ire
v ine	s ide	w ire
n ine	w ide	t ire
m ile	t ide	h ire
p ile	k ite	w ipe
t ile		
f ile		

LESSON 130: LONG O (WORD BUILDING)

The instructor:

- Reminds children that long vowels are pronounced like the name of their letter.

- Asks children to repeat the following sounds:
    1. Short o (as in *ton*)
    2. Long o (as in *tone*)

- Advises children that the *e* on the end of lesson words is silent and changes the preceding vowel from short to long.

- Displays each word, asks children to sound out each word, and allows children to decipher each word with minimal assistance.

- Recites each word aloud and directs children to:
    1. Build the word out of letter tiles.
    2. Point at each letter tile in the word while making the related sound.

long o

n o	c ore	b one
g o	t ore	c one
s o	s ore	t one
p oke	w ore	l one
j oke	m ore	p ole
y oke	d ose	h ole
h ome	r ope	m ole
d ome		s ole

LESSON 131: LONG U (WORD BUILDING)

The instructor:

- Reminds children that long vowels are pronounced like the name of their letter.

- Asks children to repeat the following sounds:
  1. Short u (as in *cut*)
  2. Long u (as in *cute*)

- Advises children that the *e* on the end of lesson words is silent and changes the preceding vowel from short to long.

- Displays each word, asks children to sound out each word, and allows children to decipher each word with minimal assistance.

- Recites each word aloud and directs children to:
  1. Build the word out of letter tiles.
  2. Point at each letter tile in the word while making the related sound.

long u

c ute   L uke
m ute   D uke
l ute   p ure
m ule   c ure
t une   l ure
J une

LESSON 132: LONG E (WORD BUILDING)

The instructor:

- Reminds children that long vowels are pronounced like the name of their letter.

- Asks children to repeat the following sounds:
    1. Short e (as in *wet*)
    2. Long e (as in *we*)

- Displays each word, asks children to sound out each word, and allows children to decipher each word with minimal assistance.

- Recites each word aloud and directs children to:
    1. Build the word out of letter tiles.
    2. Point at each letter tile in the word while making the related sound.

long e

h e

b e

w e

m e

LESSON 133: LONG VOWELS – REVIEW 1 (WORD BUILDING)

The instructor:

- Reminds children that long vowels are pronounced like the name of their letter.

- Asks children to repeat the following sounds:
    1. Long a (as in *late*)
    2. Long i (as in *hive*)
    3. Long o (as in *home*)
    4. Long u (as in *pure*)

- Advises children that the *e* on the end of lesson words is silent and changes the preceding vowel from short to long.

- Displays each word, asks children to sound out each word, and allows children to decipher each word with minimal assistance.

- Recites each word aloud and directs children to:
    1. Build the word out of letter tiles.
    2. Point at each letter tile in the word while making the related sound.

Review

late	date	pane	hope	hire
hive	bite	dive	ride	line
home	tine	wire	rode	lake
mine	robe	pile	pure	ate
mane	pole	fade	tire	bone
cape	yoke	dime	vane	pine
gave	Duke	more	wore	June
rate	cane	gate	pipe	

LESSON 134: LONG VOWELS – REVIEW 2 (WORD BUILDING)

The instructor:

- Reminds children that long vowels are pronounced like the name of their letter.

- Asks children to repeat the following sounds:
    1. Long a (as in *cake*)
    2. Long i (as in *kite*)
    3. Long o (as in *vote*)
    4. Long u (as in *mule*)

- Advises children that the *e* on the end of lesson words is silent and changes the preceding vowel from short to long.

- Displays each word, asks children to sound out each word, and allows children to decipher each word with minimal assistance.

- Recites each word aloud and directs children to:
    1. Build the word out of letter tiles.
    2. Point at each letter tile in the word while making the related sound.

Review

rake	vase	make	note	bale
ripe	core	side	tape	pale
cake	wake	wine	vine	wave
wove	hole	same	Jane	mule
tone	kite	lame	wipe	vote
rope	Kate	Luke	sale	size
time	tame	safe	cure	pave
life				

ELEMENTARY PHONICS

LESSON 135: LONG VOWELS – REVIEW 3 (WORD BUILDING)

The instructor:

- Reminds children that long vowels are pronounced like the name of their letter.
- Asks children to repeat the following sounds:
    1. Long a (as in *mate*)
    2. Long i (as in *hide*)
    3. Long o (as in *tore*)
    4. Long u (as in *use*)
    5. Long e (as in *here*)
- Advises children that the *e* on the end of lesson words is silent and changes the preceding vowel from short to long.
- Displays each word, asks children to sound out each word, and allows children to decipher each word with minimal assistance.
- Recites each word aloud and directs children to:
    1. Build the word out of letter tiles.
    2. Point at each letter tile in the word while making the related sound.

Review

sake	mate	tune	fate
use	here	dose	wife
name	wade	wide	cone
made	cave	fore	hide
nine	came	save	lane
bake	case	gaze	tore
lone	take	tide	

LESSON 136: PLURAL S FORM OF WORDS (WORD BUILDING)

The instructor:

- Reads each word and asks each child whether the word refers to one (singular) or many (plural or multiple).
    1. cat / cats
    2. cake / cakes
    3. rope / ropes
- Advises children that the *s* on the end of words often indicates more than one.
- Displays each word, asks children to sound out each word, and allows children to decipher each word with minimal assistance.
- Recites each word aloud and directs children to:
    1. Build the word out of letter tiles.
    2. Point at each letter tile in the word while making the related sound.

Plural Form

c at	n ut	r ope	w ipes	m aps
c ats	n uts	r opes	j okes	p ets
c ap	c ake	y oke	h opes	t aps
c aps	c akes	y okes	d ates	f its
s it	g ate	r akes	w ets	
s its	g ates	m akes	c ups	
d ip	p ipe	b akes	t ips	
d ips	p ipes	w akes	k ites	
t op	b ite	r ats		
t ops	b ites			

LESSON 137: PLURAL S=Z FORM OF WORDS (WORD BUILDING)

The instructor demonstrates the *z* sound, asks children to repeat the sound, and informs children sometimes *s* can sound like *z*.

For each word, the instructor:

- Displays the word, asks children to sound out the word, and allows children to decipher the word with minimal assistance.

- Recites the word aloud and directs children to:
    1. Build the word out of letter tiles.
    2. Point at each letter tile in the word while making the related sound.

s = z

as	g ames	box es
h as	t unes	six es
is	r ose	h ose
h is	r os es	w ise
p ins	n ose	r ise
l ids	n os es	r is es
r ugs	ax es	m ix es
	tax es	f use

LESSON 138: POSSESSIVE FORM OF WORDS (WORD BUILDING)

The instructor:

- Shows children the *'s* combination and informs children this combination can indicate ownership or possession.

- Gives the example that *Bill's toy* indicates the toy belongs to Bill or that Bill possesses the toy.

For each word, the instructor:

- Displays the word, asks children to sound out the word, and allows children to decipher the word with minimal assistance.

- Recites the word aloud and directs children to:
    1. Build the word out of letter tiles.
    2. Point at each letter tile in the word while making the related sound.

Possessive Form ('s)

Ned's cap	Ben's cup
Kate's rose	Sam's bat
Tom's cane	Ted's dime
Jane's cake	mule's rope
Dan's fox	cat's bed
Dave's home	hen's leg
Nat's box	man's cat
Bob's top	pig's pen

LESSON 139: COMBINATION – CK (WORD BUILDING)

The instructor:

- Tells children that when *c* and *k* are combined, their sounds may be combined into one sound.
- Points at the *ck*, makes the associated sound, and asks children to repeat the sound.

For each word, the instructor:

- Displays the word, asks children to sound out the word, and allows children to decipher the word with minimal assistance.
- Recites the word aloud and directs children to:
    1. Build the word out of letter tiles.
    2. Point at each letter tile in the word while making the related sound.

ck

b ack	p ick	l ock
l ack	l ick	r ock
p ack	k ick	b uck
s ack	s ick	d uck
t ack	d eck	l uck
	n eck	

LESSON 140: COMBINATION – LL (WORD BUILDING)

The instructor:

- Tells children that when *l* and *l* are combined, their sounds may be combined into one sound.
- Points at the *ll*, makes the associated sound, and asks children to repeat the sound.

For each word, the instructor:

- Displays the word, asks children to sound out the word, and allows children to decipher the word with minimal assistance.
- Recites the word aloud and directs children to:
    1. Build the word out of letter tiles.
    2. Point at each letter tile in the word while making the related sound.

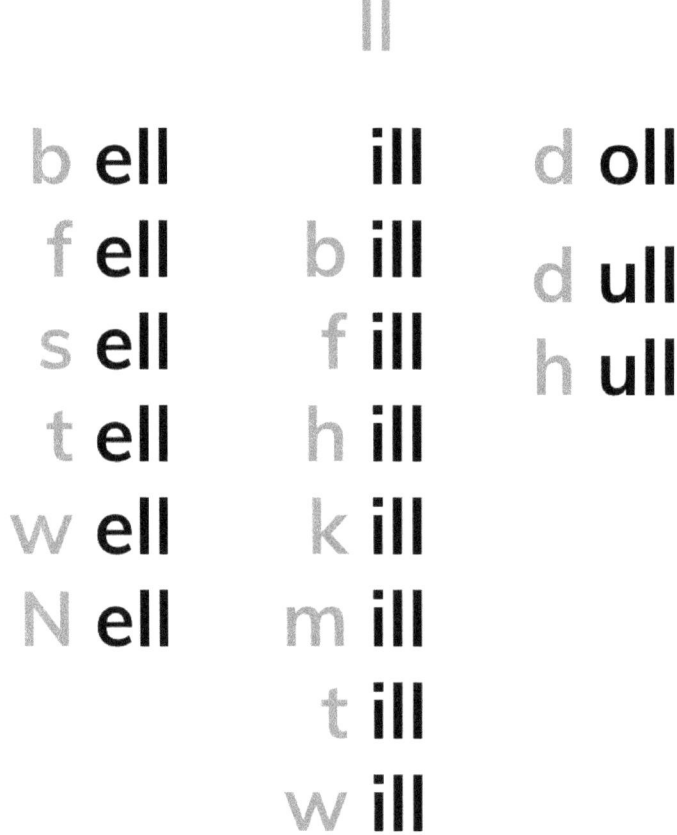

LESSON 141: COMBINATIONS – SS/FF/ZZ (WORD BUILDING)

The instructor:

- Tells children that when *s* and *s* are combined, their sounds may be combined into one sound.
- Points at the *ss*, makes the associated sound, and asks children to repeat the sound.
- Repeats the above instructions for *ff* and *zz*.

For each word, the instructor:

- Displays the word, asks children to sound out the word, and allows children to decipher the word with minimal assistance.
- Recites the word aloud and directs children to:
    1. Build the word out of letter tiles.
    2. Point at each letter tile in the word while making the related sound.

ss	ff	zz
l ess	b uff	f uzz
B ess	r uff	b uzz
h iss	c uff	
k iss	m uff	
m iss	p uff	
f uss		
m uss		

LESSON 142: SHORT VOWEL FOLLOWED BY 2 CONSONANTS – PART 1 (WORD BUILDING)

The instructor tells children the lesson words follow a common pattern – a *short vowel* is followed by two dissimilar consonants.

For each word, the instructor:

- Displays the word, asks children to sound out the word, and allows children to decipher the word with minimal assistance.
- Recites the word aloud and directs children to:
    1. Build the word out of letter tiles.
    2. Point at each letter tile in the word while making the related sound.

and	m end	h int
h and	s end	l int
l and	b ent	m int
s and	r ent	t int
b and	s ent	h unt
end	t ent	w ind
b end	w ent	p ond

LESSON 143: SHORT VOWEL FOLLOWED BY 2 CONSONANTS – PART 2 (WORD BUILDING)

The instructor tells children the lesson words follow a common pattern – a *short vowel* is followed by two dissimilar consonants.

For each word, the instructor:

- Displays the word, asks children to sound out the word, and allows children to decipher the word with minimal assistance.
- Recites the word aloud and directs children to:
    1. Build the word out of letter tiles.
    2. Point at each letter tile in the word while making the related sound.

w est	m ust	b ump
b est	d ust	p ump
v est	r ust	d ump
n est	j ust	j ump
t est	d amp	l ump
r est	c amp	r omp
l ist	l amp	n ext
f ish	l imp	t ext
m ist		

LESSON 144: SHORT VOWEL FOLLOWED BY 2 CONSONANTS – PART 3 (WORD BUILDING)

The instructor tells children the lesson words follow a common pattern – a *short vowel* is followed by two dissimilar consonants.

For each word, the instructor:

- Displays the word, asks children to sound out the word, and allows children to decipher the word with minimal assistance.
- Recites the word aloud and directs children to:
    1. Build the word out of letter tiles.
    2. Point at each letter tile in the word while making the related sound.

b elt	m ilk	w ilt
f elt	s ilk	g ift
m elt	h elp	l ift
s elf	y elp	r ift
b ulk	k ept	s ift
el k	w ept	

LESSON 145: MISCELLANEOUS – REVIEW (WORD BUILDING)

The instructor tells children the lesson words follow a common pattern – a *short vowel* is followed by two consonants.

For each word, the instructor:

- Displays the word, asks children to sound out the word, and allows children to decipher the word with minimal assistance.
- Recites the word aloud and directs children to:
    1. Build the word out of letter tiles.
    2. Point at each letter tile in the word while making the related sound.

Review

left	send	hand
huff	tilt	sift
hemp	hint	lend
went	west	hiss
less	romp	held
Jack	Bess	add
Jill	wick	Bell
next	pump	dent
mock	Dick	Bill

LESSON 146: COMBINATION – CH (WORD BUILDING)

The instructor:

- Tells children that when *c* and *h* are combined, their sounds may be combined into a new sound.
- Points at the *ch*, makes the associated sound, and asks children to repeat the sound.

For each word, the instructor:

- Displays the word, asks children to sound out the word, and allows children to decipher the word with minimal assistance.
- Recites the word aloud and directs children to:
    1. Build the word out of letter tiles.
    2. Point at each letter tile in the word while making the related sound.

ch

ch ime	ch ill	l un ch
ch ick	ch afe	b un ch
ch oke	ch ip	p un ch
ch in	ch at	s u ch
ch ap	ch op	m u ch
ch ase	ch ose	ri ch
ch eck		ben ch

LESSON 147: COMBINATION – TCH=CH (WORD BUILDING)

The instructor:

- Informs children that when *t*, *c*, and *h* are combined, their sounds may be combined into a new sound.
- Tells children the *t* is silent in the combination *tch*, and points out that in these words, *tch* sounds like *ch*.
- Points at the *tch*, makes the associated sound, and asks children to repeat the sound.

For each word, the instructor:

- Displays the word, asks children to sound out the word, and allows children to decipher the word with minimal assistance.
- Recites the word aloud and directs children to:
    1. Build the word out of letter tiles.
    2. Point at each letter tile in the word while making the related sound.

tch = ch

patch	pitch	notch
latch	hitch	botch
catch	ditch	Dutch
hatch		
match		

LESSON 148: COMBINATION – SH PART 1 (WORD BUILDING)

The instructor:

- Tells children that when *s* and *h* are combined, their sounds may be combined into a new sound.
- Points at the *sh*, makes the associated sound, and asks children to repeat the sound.

For each word, the instructor:

- Displays the word, asks children to sound out the word, and allows children to decipher the word with minimal assistance.
- Recites the word aloud and directs children to:
    1. Build the word out of letter tiles.
    2. Point at each letter tile in the word while making the related sound.

sh

sh ade	sh ine	sh un
sh ake	sh ip	sh ut
sh all	sh ock	sh ave
sh ame	sh od	sh rub
sh ape	sh one	sh rill
sh ed	sh ot	sh rimp
sh ell	sh ore	sh red
sh elf	sh op	sh rug

LESSON 149: COMBINATION – SH PART 2 (WORD BUILDING)

The instructor:

- Tells children that when *s* and *h* are combined, their sounds may be combined into a new sound.
- Points at the *sh*, makes the associated sound, and asks children to repeat the sound.

For each word, the instructor:

- Displays the word, asks children to sound out the word, and allows children to decipher the word with minimal assistance.
- Recites the word aloud and directs children to:
  1. Build the word out of letter tiles.
  2. Point at each letter tile in the word while making the related sound.

sh

a sh   di sh
ca sh   wi sh
da sh   fi sh
la sh   hu sh
ma sh   ru sh
sa sh

LESSON 150: COMBINATION – VOICELESS TH (WORD BUILDING)

The instructor:

- Informs children *voiceless th* sounds (as in *thick*) are made without using the vocal cords.
- Tells children that when *t* and *h* are combined, their sounds are combined into a new sound.
- Points at the *th*, makes the associated sound, and asks children to repeat the sound.

For each word, the instructor:

- Displays the word, asks children to sound out the word, and allows children to decipher the word with minimal assistance.
- Recites the word aloud and directs children to:
  1. Build the word out of letter tiles.
  2. Point at each letter tile in the word while making the related sound.

"voiceless" th

th in	th rone	wid th
th ick	th rash	ten th
th ump	th rush	wi th
th rill	th rust	
th rob	th rift	
th rive		

LESSON 151: COMBINATION – VOICED TH (WORD BUILDING)

The instructor:

- Informs children *voiced th* (as in *the*) sounds are made using the vocal cords.
- Tells children that when *t* and *h* are combined, their sounds are combined into a new sound.
- Points at the *th*, makes the associated sound, and asks children to repeat the sound.

For each word, the instructor:

- Displays the word, asks children to sound out the word, and allows children to decipher the word with minimal assistance.
- Recites the word aloud and directs children to:
    1. Build the word out of letter tiles.
    2. Point at each letter tile in the word while making the related sound.

"voiced" th

th e	th ose
th at	th em
th en	th us
th is	th ine
th ese	th an

LESSON 152: COMBINATION – WH (WORD BUILDING)

The instructor:

- Tells children that when *w* and *h* are combined, their sounds may be combined into a new sound.
- Points at the *wh*, makes the associated sound, and asks children to repeat the sound.

For each word, the instructor:

- Displays the word, asks children to sound out the word, and allows children to decipher the word with minimal assistance.
- Recites the word aloud and directs children to:
    1. Build the word out of letter tiles.
    2. Point at each letter tile in the word while making the related sound.

wh

wh ip	wh iff
wh ale	wh ile
wh en	wh ack
wh et	wh ite
wh ich	wh im
wh ine	wh iz

LESSON 153: MISCELLANEOUS – REVIEW (WORD BUILDING)

The instructor reviews the sounds of *ch*, *sh*, *voiceless th*, *voiced th*, and *wh*, makes each sound, and asks children to repeat each sound.

For each word, the instructor:

- Displays the word, asks children to sound out the word, and allows children to decipher the word with minimal assistance.
- Recites the word aloud and directs children to:
    1. Build the word out of letter tiles.
    2. Point at each letter tile in the word while making the related sound.

Review

chores	whine	thrush
shake	chill	shuck
thatch	mush	chop
which	with	then
shift	shade	chest
this	these	shrill

LESSON 154: COMBINATIONS – BL/CL/FL (WORD BUILDING)

The instructor:

- Points at the *bl*, makes the associated sound, and asks children to repeat the sound.
- Repeats the above instructions for *cl* and *fl*.

For each word, the instructor:

- Displays the word, asks children to sound out the word, and allows children to decipher the word with minimal assistance.
- Recites the word aloud and directs children to:
  1. Build the word out of letter tiles.
  2. Point at each letter tile in the word while making the related sound.

bl	cl	fl
bl ack	cl ose	fl ame
bl ade	cl ick	fl ag
bl ame	cl ock	fl ake
bl aze	cl uck	fl at
bl ed	cl am	fl ax
bl ess	cl ap	fl esh
bl ock	cl ip	fl it
bl ot	cl od	fl ock
bl uff	cl ub	fl op
bl unt	cl utch	fl ash
bl ush	cl ove	fl ume

LESSON 155: COMBINATIONS – SL/PL/GL (WORD BUILDING)

The instructor:

- Points at the *sl*, makes the associated sound, and asks children to repeat the sound.
- Repeats the above instructions for *pl* and *gl*.

For each word, the instructor:

- Displays the word, asks children to sound out the word, and allows children to decipher the word with minimal assistance.
- Recites the word aloud and directs children to:
    1. Build the word out of letter tiles.
    2. Point at each letter tile in the word while making the related sound.

sl

- sl ack
- sl ab
- sl ash
- sl am
- sl at
- sl ate
- sl ave
- sl ed
- sl ip

- sl id
- sl it
- sl im
- sl ime
- sl ide
- sl ope
- sl ush
- sl ug

pl

- pl ate
- pl an
- pl ant
- pl ot
- pl um
- pl ume
- pl ush

gl

- gl aze
- gl ad
- gl ade
- gl ass
- gl ide
- gl obe

LESSON 156: COMBINATION – SP (WORD BUILDING)

The instructor points at the *sp*, makes the associated sound, and asks children to repeat the sound.

For each word, the instructor:
- Displays the word, asks children to sound out the word, and allows children to decipher the word with minimal assistance.
- Recites the word aloud and directs children to:
    1. Build the word out of letter tiles.
    2. Point at each letter tile in the word while making the related sound.

sp

sp lash	sp end	sp un
sp lit	sp ill	sp ike
sp lint	sp in	sp ire
sp ade	sp ine	sp ite
sp an	sp oke	wi sp
sp eck	sp ot	li sp
sp ell		

LESSON 157: COMBINATIONS – BR/CR (WORD BUILDING)

The instructor:

- Points at the *br*, makes the associated sound, and asks children to repeat the sound.
- Repeats the above instructions for *cr*.

For each word, the instructor:

- Displays the word, asks children to sound out the word, and allows children to decipher the word with minimal assistance.
- Recites the word aloud and directs children to:
    1. Build the word out of letter tiles.
    2. Point at each letter tile in the word while making the related sound.

br

br an	br ide
br ag	br im
br ake	br oke
br ave	br ush
br ick	br ine

cr

cr ab	cr ept
cr ack	cr ib
cr ate	cr ush
cr ane	cr ock
cr op	cr ust
cr amp	cr imp
cr isp	

LESSON 158: COMBINATIONS – SC/SK (WORD BUILDING)

The instructor:

- Points at the *sc*, makes the associated sound, and asks children to repeat the sound.

- Repeats the above instructions for *sk* and notes that *sc* and *sk* have the same sound in the words listed below.

For each word, the instructor:

- Displays the word, asks children to sound out the word, and allows children to decipher the word with minimal assistance.

- Recites the word aloud and directs children to:
    1. Build the word out of letter tiles.
    2. Point at each letter tile in the word while making the related sound.

sc

sc rap	sc ale
sc rape	sc ant
sc ratch	sc ore
sc rub	sc um
sc amp	Sc otch
sc at	

sk

sk ate	ri sk
sk etch	bri sk
sk iff	hu sk
sk ill	du sk
sk ull	mu sk
sk ip	tu sk
sk im	
sk in	

LESSON 159: COMBINATIONS – DR/FR/SPR (WORD BUILDING)

The instructor:

- Points at the *dr*, makes the associated sound, and asks children to repeat the sound.
- Repeats the above instructions for *fr* and *spr*.

For each word, the instructor:

- Displays the word, asks children to sound out the word, and allows children to decipher the word with minimal assistance.
- Recites the word aloud and directs children to:
    1. Build the word out of letter tiles.
    2. Point at each letter tile in the word while making the related sound.

dr

dr ag	dr ove		
dr ess	dr ug		
dr ift	dr um		
dr ill	dr ip		
dr ive	dr ape		
dr op	dr one		

fr

fr ame	fr og
fr et	fr ock
fr esh	fr om
Fr ench	fr isk
fr ill	fr oze

spr

spr ig
spr ite

LESSON 160: COMBINATIONS – GR/PR/TR (WORD BUILDING)

The instructor:

- Points at the *gr*, makes the associated sound, and asks children to repeat the sound.
- Repeats the above instructions for *pr* and *tr*.

For each word, the instructor:

- Displays the word, asks children to sound out the word, and allows children to decipher the word with minimal assistance.
- Recites the word aloud and directs children to:
    1. Build the word out of letter tiles.
    2. Point at each letter tile in the word while making the related sound.

gr		pr	tr	
gr ade	gr ip	pr ess	tr ack	tr ill
gr and	gr it	pr ide	tr act	tr im
gr aze	gr ill	pr ize	tr amp	tr ip
gr ate	gr in	pr op	tr ash	tr od
gr ave	gr ove	pr ose	tr ap	tr ot
gr ape	gr unt	pr int	tr ade	tr uck
			tr ick	

LESSON 161: COMBINATIONS – ST/STE (WORD BUILDING)

The instructor:

- Points at the *st*, makes the associated sound, and asks children to repeat the sound.

- Repeats the above instructions for *ste*, notes that the *e* is silent, and that in the words below, *st* and *ste* sound alike.

For each word, the instructor:

- Displays the word, asks children to sound out the word, and allows children to decipher the word with minimal assistance.

- Recites the word aloud and directs children to:
    1. Build the word out of letter tiles.
    2. Point at each letter tile in the word while making the related sound.

st / ste

st rip	st ake	st ill	cre st
st ripe	st ale	st ilt	che st
st rive	st amp	st itch	le st
st retch	st omp	st ole	ble st
st rict	st ump	st ove	cru st
st ride	st and	st one	tru st
st rike	st ate	st op	ha ste
st rap	st ep	st ub	pa ste
st roke	st em	st uck	ta ste
st ab	st ick	st uff	wa ste
st ack	st iff	st ore	ba ste

LESSON 162: COMBINATIONS – SM/SN/SW (WORD BUILDING)

The instructor:

- Points at the *sm*, makes the associated sound, and asks children to repeat the sound.
- Repeats the above instructions for *sn* and *sw*.

For each word, the instructor:

- Displays the word, asks children to sound out the word, and allows children to decipher the word with minimal assistance.
- Recites the word aloud and directs children to:
    1. Build the word out of letter tiles.
    2. Point at each letter tile in the word while making the related sound.

sm	sn	sw
sm ell	sn ake	sw ell
sm elt	sn ap	sw ept
sm ash	sn atch	sw im
sm ile	sn iff	sw am
sm ith	sn uff	sw um
sm oke	sn ipe	sw ine
sm ack	sn ore	sw itch
	sn ug	sw ore
	sn ag	sw ift

LESSON 163: COMBINATIONS – TW/QU (WORD BUILDING)

The instructor:

- Points at the *tw*, makes the associated sound, and asks children to repeat the sound.
- Repeats the above instructions for *qu*, reminding children that *q* tends to be paired with *u*.

For each word, the instructor:

- Displays the word, asks children to sound out the word, and allows children to decipher the word with minimal assistance.
- Recites the word aloud and directs children to:
  1. Build the word out of letter tiles.
  2. Point at each letter tile in the word while making the related sound.

tw	qu
tw ine	qu ack
tw ig	qu ill
tw ill	qu ilt
tw ist	qu it
tw it	qu ite
tw itch	qu iz
tw ins	qu ick
	s qu int

LESSON 164: MISCELLANEOUS – REVIEW (WORD BUILDING)

For each word, the instructor:

- Displays the word, asks children to sound out the word, and allows children to decipher the word with minimal assistance.
- Recites the word aloud and directs children to:
  1. Build the word out of letter tiles.
  2. Point at each letter tile in the word while making the related sound.

Review

blend	quench	scrape
stripe	crust	clamp
broke	trade	sprig
fleck	frame	risk
slide	twist	flap
stitch	spend	snatch
drape	grim	scamp
smile	fluff	splash
print	skate	swift

LESSON 165: THREE SOUNDS OF Y – PART 1 (WORD BUILDING)

The instructor points at the *y*, makes the associated sound (as in *yes*), and asks children to repeat the sound.

For each word, the instructor:

- Displays the word, asks children to sound out the word, and allows children to decipher the word with minimal assistance.
- Recites the word aloud and directs children to:
    1. Build the word out of letter tiles.
    2. Point at each letter tile in the word while making the related sound.

y

y es

y et

y ell

y elp

Y ale

y oke

LESSON 166: THREE SOUNDS OF Y – PART 2 (WORD BUILDING)

The instructor:

- Tells children that in the lesson words, *y* sounds like *long e*.
- Points at the *y*, makes the associated sound, and asks children to repeat the sound.

For each word, the instructor:

- Displays the word, asks children to sound out the word, and allows children to decipher the word with minimal assistance.
- Recites the word aloud and directs children to:
  1. Build the word out of letter tiles.
  2. Point at each letter tile in the word while making the related sound.

y = long e

candy	puppy	fluffy
cherry	carry	funny
merry	empty	jolly
windy	dusty	foggy
kitty	twenty	Betty
penny	fifty	Henry
chilly	sixty	Bunny
sorry	ninety	Polly
sunny	copy	

LESSON 167: THREE SOUNDS OF Y – PART 3 (WORD BUILDING)

The instructor:

- Tells children that in lesson words, *y* sounds like *long i*.
- Points at the *y*, makes the associated sound, and asks children to repeat the sound.

For each word, the instructor:

- Displays the word, asks children to sound out the word, and allows children to decipher the word with minimal assistance.
- Recites the word aloud and directs children to:
    1. Build the word out of letter tiles.
    2. Point at each letter tile in the word while making the related sound.

y = long i

by	spy
my	thy
cry	try
dry	why
fly	rye
fry	shy
pry	sky
sly	style

LESSON 168: COMBINATION – AI=LONG A (WORD BUILDING)

The instructor:

- Tells children that when two vowels come together, the first is usually long and the second is typically silent.
- Informs children that in the lesson words, *ai* sounds like *long a* and the *i* is silent.
- Points at the *ai*, makes the associated sound, and asks children to repeat the sound.

For each word, the instructor:

- Displays the word, asks children to sound out the word, and allows children to decipher the word with minimal assistance.
- Recites the word aloud and directs children to:
    1. Build the word out of letter tiles.
    2. Point at each letter tile in the word while making the related sound.

ai = long a

aid	hail	aim	sprain	paint
laid	jail	claim	main	quaint
maid	mail	gain	pain	raise
paid	nail	rain	lain	praise
braid	sail	drain	plain	waist
ail	snail	brain	slain	bait
fail	pail	grain	chain	gait
bail	tail	train	stain	wait
rail	trail	strain	faint	strait

LESSON 169: COMBINATION – AY=LONG A (WORD BUILDING)

The instructor:

- Tells children that when two vowels come together, the first is usually long and the second is typically silent.
- Informs children that in the lesson words, *ay* sounds like *long a* and the *y* is silent.
- Points at the *ay*, makes the associated sound, and asks children to repeat the sound.

For each word, the instructor:

- Displays the word, asks children to sound out the word, and allows children to decipher the word with minimal assistance.
- Recites the word aloud and directs children to:
    1. Build the word out of letter tiles.
    2. Point at each letter tile in the word while making the related sound.

ay = long a

b ay	hay	say
d ay	lay	stay
r ay	clay	stray
tr ay	may	way
g ay	pay	pray
gray	play	

LESSON 170: COMBINATION – EA=LONG E PART 1 (WORD BUILDING)

The instructor:

- Tells children that when two vowels come together, the first is usually long and the second is typically silent.
- Informs children that in the lesson words, *ea* sounds like *long e* and the *a* is silent.
- Points at the *ea*, makes the associated sound, and asks children to repeat the sound.

For each word, the instructor:

- Displays the word, asks children to sound out the word, and allows children to decipher the word with minimal assistance.
- Recites the word aloud and directs children to:
  1. Build the word out of letter tiles.
  2. Point at each letter tile in the word while making the related sound.

ea = long e

s ea	lead	sneak	team
t ea	read	squeak	steam
fl ea	leaf	heal	stream
ea ch	leak	meal	dream
b each	beak	seal	bean
peach	peak	squeal	lean
reach	speak	steal	mean
teach	weak	beam	clean
bead	streak	seam	heap

LESSON 171: COMBINATION – EA=LONG E PART 2 (WORD BUILDING)

The instructor:

- Tells children that when two vowels come together, the first is usually long and the second is typically silent.
- Informs children that in the lesson words, *ea* sounds like *long e* and the *a* is silent.
- Points at the *ea*, makes the associated sound, and asks children to repeat the sound.

For each word, the instructor:

- Displays the word, asks children to sound out the word, and allows children to decipher the word with minimal assistance.
- Recites the word aloud and directs children to:
    1. Build the word out of letter tiles.
    2. Point at each letter tile in the word while making the related sound.

ea = long e

leap	year	beast	seat
cheap	clear	feast	cheat
reap	shear	yeast	treat
ear	ease	eat	wheat
fear	easy	beat	eaves
hear	tease	heat	leave
near	please	meat	heave
tear	east	neat	weave
dear			

LESSON 172: COMBINATION – EE=LONG E PART 1 (WORD BUILDING)

The instructor:

- Tells children that in the lesson words, *ee* sounds like *long e*.
- Points at the *ee*, makes the associated sound, and asks children to repeat the sound.

For each word, the instructor:

- Displays the word, asks children to sound out the word, and allows children to decipher the word with minimal assistance.
- Recites the word aloud and directs children to:
  1. Build the word out of letter tiles.
  2. Point at each letter tile in the word while making the related sound.

ee = long e

see	speech	deed	bleed
fee	screech	feed	reed
bee	three	need	greed
flee	tree	seed	beef
free	beech	weed	reef
glee	leech		

LESSON 173: COMBINATION – EE=LONG E PART 2 (WORD BUILDING)

The instructor:

- Tells children that in the lesson words, *ee* sounds like *long e*.
- Points at the *ee*, makes the associated sound, and asks children to repeat the sound.

For each word, the instructor:

- Displays the word, asks children to sound out the word, and allows children to decipher the word with minimal assistance.
- Recites the word aloud and directs children to:
    1. Build the word out of letter tiles.
    2. Point at each letter tile in the word while making the related sound.

ee = long e

seek	feel	seem	sheen
week	heel	seen	deep
cheek	keel	screen	keep
creek	peel	keen	sheep
meek	reel	queen	steep
eel	steel		

LESSON 174: COMBINATION – EE=LONG E PART 3 (WORD BUILDING)

The instructor:

- Tells children that in the lesson words, *ee* sounds like *long e*.
- Points at the *ee*, makes the associated sound, and asks children to repeat the sound.

For each word, the instructor:

- Displays the word, asks children to sound out the word, and allows children to decipher the word with minimal assistance.
- Recites the word aloud and directs children to:
    1. Build the word out of letter tiles.
    2. Point at each letter tile in the word while making the related sound.

ee = long e

sweep	beet	fleet
creep	feet	greet
sleep	meet	breeze
peep	sheet	freeze
deer	sweet	sneeze
cheer	street	squeeze

LESSON 175: COMBINATION – IE=LONG I (WORD BUILDING)

The instructor:

- Tells children that when two vowels come together, the first is usually long and the second is typically silent.

- Informs children that in the lesson words, *ie* sounds like *long i* and the *e* is silent.

- Points at the *ie*, makes the associated sound, and asks children to repeat the sound.

For each word, the instructor:

- Displays the word, asks children to sound out the word, and allows children to decipher the word with minimal assistance.

- Recites the word aloud and directs children to:
    1. Build the word out of letter tiles.
    2. Point at each letter tile in the word while making the related sound.

ie = long i

die

lie

fie

pie

tie

LESSON 176: COMBINATION – OA=LONG O PART 1 (WORD BUILDING)

The instructor:

- Tells children that when two vowels come together, the first is usually long and the second is typically silent.
- Informs children that in the lesson words, *oa* sounds like *long o* and the *a* is silent.
- Points at the *oa*, makes the associated sound, and asks children to repeat the sound.

For each word, the instructor:

- Displays the word, asks children to sound out the word, and allows children to decipher the word with minimal assistance.
- Recites the word aloud and directs children to:
    1. Build the word out of letter tiles.
    2. Point at each letter tile in the word while making the related sound.

oa = long o

l oad	roach	goal
r oad	oak	foam
t oad	cloak	roam
l oaf	croak	groan
c oach	soak	loan
poach	coal	moan

LESSON 177: COMBINATION – OA=LONG O PART 2 (WORD BUILDING)

The instructor:

- Tells children that when two vowels come together, the first is usually long and the second is typically silent.
- Informs children that in the lesson words, *oa* sounds like *long o* and the *a* is silent.
- Points at the *oa*, makes the associated sound, and asks children to repeat the sound.

For each word, the instructor:

- Displays the word, asks children to sound out the word, and allows children to decipher the word with minimal assistance.
- Recites the word aloud and directs children to:
    1. Build the word out of letter tiles.
    2. Point at each letter tile in the word while making the related sound.

oa = long o

soap	throat	hoarse
oat	oar	roast
coat	soar	toast
float	roar	coast
goat	board	boast
boat	coarse	

LESSON 178: COMBINATIONS – OE=LONG O AND UE=LONG U (WORD BUILDING)

The instructor:

- Tells children that when two vowels come together, the first is usually long and the second is typically silent.
- Informs children that in the lesson words, *oe* sounds like *long o* and the *e* is silent.
- Points at the *oe*, makes the associated sound, and asks children to repeat the sound.
- Repeats the above instructions for *ue*.

For each word, the instructor:

- Displays the word, asks children to sound out the word, and allows children to decipher the word with minimal assistance.
- Recites the word aloud and directs children to:
    1. Build the word out of letter tiles.
    2. Point at each letter tile in the word while making the related sound.

oe = long o   ue = long u

t oe	s ue
w oe	c ue
hoe	hue
foe	due

LESSON 179: ADDITIONAL LONG I WORDS (WORD BUILDING)

The instructor points at the *long i*, makes the associated sound, and asks children to repeat the sound.

For each word, the instructor:

- Displays the word, asks children to sound out the word, and allows children to decipher the word with minimal assistance.
- Recites each word aloud and directs children to:
  1. Build the word out of letter tiles.
  2. Point at each letter tile in the word while making the related sound.

long i

mild	grind
wild	hind
child	kind
bind	mind
blind	wind
find	

LESSON 180: COMBINATION – IGH=LONG I (WORD BUILDING)

The instructor:

- Tells children that in the lesson words, *igh* sounds like *long i*.
- Points at the *igh*, makes the associated sound, and asks children to repeat the sound.

For each word, the instructor:

- Displays the word, asks children to sound out the word, and allows children to decipher the word with minimal assistance.
- Recites the word aloud and directs children to:
    1. Build the word out of letter tiles.
    2. Point at each letter tile in the word while making the related sound.

igh = long i

s igh	night
s ight	right
fight	tight
might	bright
high	flight
light	

LESSON 181: ADDITIONAL LONG O WORDS (WORD BUILDING)

The instructor points at the *long o*, makes the associated sound, and asks children to repeat the sound.

For each word, the instructor:

- Displays the word, asks children to sound out the word, and allows children to decipher the word with minimal assistance.
- Recites the word aloud and directs children to:
    1. Build the word out of letter tiles.
    2. Point at each letter tile in the word while making the related sound.

long o

old	sold	most	torn
told	scold	colt	worn
cold	roll	jolt	porch
gold	toll	bolt	forth
hold	stroll	pork	both
mold	post		

LESSON 182: COMBINATION – OW (WORD BUILDING)

The instructor:

- Tells children that in the lesson words, *ow* sounds like the *ow* in *cow*.
- Points at the *ow*, makes the associated sound, and asks children to repeat the sound.

For each word, the instructor:

- Displays the word, asks children to sound out the word, and allows children to decipher the word with minimal assistance.
- Recites the word aloud and directs children to:
    1. Build the word out of letter tiles.
    2. Point at each letter tile in the word while making the related sound.

ow

ow l	how	frown
h owl	now	crown
fowl	plow	brown
scowl	down	drown
growl	town	crowd
brow	gown	drowsy
cow	clown	bow

LESSON 183: COMBINATION – OU=OW (WORD BUILDING)

The instructor:

- Tells children that in the lesson words, *ou* sounds like the *ow* in *cow*.
- Points at the *ou*, makes the associated sound, and asks children to repeat the sound.

For each word, the instructor:

- Displays the word, asks children to sound out the word, and allows children to decipher the word with minimal assistance.
- Recites the word aloud and directs children to:
    1. Build the word out of letter tiles.
    2. Point at each letter tile in the word while making the related sound.

ou = ow

couch	mound	sour	pout
crouch	pound	scour	spout
pouch	round	flour	sprout
slouch	ground	house	stout
loud	sound	mouse	trout
cloud	wound	grouse	shout
proud	count	blouse	mouth
bound	mount	out	south
found	our		

LESSON 184: COMBINATION – OW=LONG O (WORD BUILDING)

The instructor:

- Tells children that in the lesson words, *ow* sounds like the *long o* in *bowl*.
- Points at the *ow*, makes the associated sound, and asks children to repeat the sound.

For each word, the instructor:

- Displays the word, asks children to sound out the word, and allows children to decipher the word with minimal assistance.
- Recites the word aloud and directs children to:
    1. Build the word out of letter tiles.
    2. Point at each letter tile in the word while making the related sound.

ow = long o

owe	show	flown
bow	snow	thrown
low	throw	growth
blow	stow	yellow
flow	bowl	window
row	own	elbow
grow	mown	hollow
glow	sown	mellow
crow	blown	widow
mow	grown	shadow

LESSON 185: COMBINATION – OU=LONG O (WORD BUILDING)

The instructor:

- Tells children that in the lesson words, *ou* sounds like the *long o* in *four*.
- Points at the *ou*, makes the associated *long o* sound, and asks children to repeat the sound.

For each word, the instructor:

- Displays the word, asks children to sound out the word, and allows children to decipher the word with minimal assistance.
- Recites the word aloud and directs children to:
  1. Build the word out of letter tiles.
  2. Point at each letter tile in the word while making the related sound.

ou = long o

four
pour
court
course
soul

LESSON 186: COMBINATIONS – ING/INGS (WORD BUILDING)

The instructor:

- Points at the *ing*, makes the associated sound, and asks children to repeat the sound.
- Repeats the instructions for *ings* as in *rings*.

For each word, the instructor:

- Displays the word, asks children to sound out the word, and allows children to decipher the word with minimal assistance.
- Recites the word aloud and directs children to:
  1. Build the word out of letter tiles.
  2. Point at each letter tile in the word while making the related sound.

ing ings

k ing	string	swing	cling
k ings	strings	swings	clings
r ing	sling	spring	thing
r ings	slings	springs	things
s ing	wing	bring	
s ings	wings	brings	

LESSON 187: COMBINATION – ING IN TWO-SYLLABLE WORDS (WORD BUILDING)

The instructor points at the *ing*, makes the associated sounds, and asks children to repeat the sounds.

For each word, the instructor:

- Displays the word, asks children to sound out the word, and allows children to decipher the word with minimal assistance.

- Recites the word aloud and directs children to:
  1. Build the word out of letter tiles.
  2. Point at each letter tile in the word while making the related sound.

ing

matting	bending	throwing	meeting
running	hunting	singing	loaning
boxing	resting	bringing	lightning
rubbing	jumping	fretting	folding
mixing	pouring	trying	rolling
packing	helping	braiding	plowing
filling	adding	minding	counting
puffing	wishing	playing	flowing
buzzing	spending	reading	steering

LESSON 188: COMBINATION – ER (WORD BUILDING)

The instructor points at the *er*, makes the associated sounds, and asks children to repeat the sounds.

For each word, the instructor:

- Displays the word, asks children to sound out the word, and allows children to decipher the word with minimal assistance.
- Recites the word aloud and directs children to:
  1. Build the word out of letter tiles.
  2. Point at each letter tile in the word while making the related sound.

er

her	temper	rocker	browner
were	term	wilder	grayer
jerk	better	Easter	bitter
nerve	rubber	miller	upper
perch	deeper	grinder	tender
fern	thunder	counter	singer
verse	older	sleeper	servant
ever	colder	teacher	timber
stern	dinner	sifter	brighter

LESSON 189: COMBINATION – ERS (WORD BUILDING)

The instructor:

- Reviews the sound of *er*.
- Points at the *ers*, makes the associated sounds, and asks children to repeat the sounds.
- Reminds children that the *s* on the end of words often indicates more than one.

For each word, the instructor:

- Displays the word, asks children to sound out the word, and allows children to decipher the word with minimal assistance.
- Recites the word aloud and directs children to:
  1. Build the word out of letter tiles.
  2. Point at each letter tile in the word while making the related sound.

er ers

sister	painter	owner
sisters	painters	owners
flower	cracker	roller
flowers	crackers	rollers
winter	pitcher	hammer
winters	pitchers	hammers

LESSON 190: MISCELLANEOUS – REVIEW 1 (WORD BUILDING)

For each word, the instructor:

- Displays the word, asks children to sound out the word, and allows children to decipher the word with minimal assistance.

- Recites the word aloud and directs children to:
    1. Build the word out of letter tiles.
    2. Point at each letter tile in the word while making the related sound.

Review

skip	bunch	sling	sketch
creek	snail	beet	snow
grain	spring	foggy	grape
might	flyer	graze	roller
mint	speak	ore	slush
soak	strike	power	night
mine	lye	bowl	totter
cream	please	told	failing
roaring	leaf	fear	gray
chase	swell	ground	prize
owe	perch	woe	meaning

ELEMENTARY PHONICS

LESSON 191: MISCELLANEOUS – REVIEW 2 (WORD BUILDING)

For each word, the instructor:

- Displays the word, asks children to sound out the word, and allows children to decipher the word with minimal assistance.
- Recites the word aloud and directs children to:
    1. Build the word out of letter tiles.
    2. Point at each letter tile in the word while making the related sound.

Review

bone	cloth	mopping
shift	follow	stretch
supper	jail	sand
trust	spins	peach
sorrow	coal	patter
perch	smear	glad
off	raise	clinch
four	blade	bench
suppose	socks	weaker
clings	drugs	offer
wades	throat	scolding
greedy	flesh	

LESSON 192: MISCELLANEOUS – REVIEW 3 (WORD BUILDING)

For each word, the instructor:

- Displays the word, asks children to sound out the word, and allows children to decipher the word with minimal assistance.
- Recites the word aloud and directs children to:
    1. Build the word out of letter tiles.
    2. Point at each letter tile in the word while making the related sound.

Review

west	thrush	feeds	sniffs
flock	stand	stake	tried
shaggy	plump	cheese	teeth
house	twine	times	wing
still	blister	swept	hack
Jack's	June	cheek	cost
leader	shelf	trench	smile
snake	wetter	ever	toss
froth	sweep	fish	study
post	pills	shells	splash
whiz	slope	bluff	street
cores			

LESSON 193: MISCELLANEOUS – REVIEW 4 (WORD BUILDING)

For each word, the instructor:
- Displays the word, asks children to sound out the word, and allows children to decipher the word with minimal assistance.
- Recites the word aloud and directs children to:
  1. Build the word out of letter tiles.
  2. Point at each letter tile in the word while making the related sound.

Review

shadow	close	preach
snatch	mouse	sleeve
trout	twelfth	toast
crust	dray	May's
vote	oaks	crown
stitch	frills	style
kind	coats	teams
twig	cherry	pillow
clerk	saves	breeze
sweets	frosty	lamp
pepper	feelers	brain

LESSON 194: COMBINATIONS – ANG/ONG/UNG/ENG (WORD BUILDING)

The instructor:

- Points at the *ang*, makes the associated sound, and asks children to repeat the sound.

- Repeats the instructions for *ong*, *ung*, and *eng*.

For each word, the instructor:

- Displays the word, asks children to sound out the word, and allows children to decipher the word with minimal assistance.

- Recites the word aloud and directs children to:
    1. Build the word out of letter tiles.
    2. Point at each letter tile in the word while making the related sound.

ang	ong	ung	eng
bang	song	hung	length
hang	songs	rung	strength
hanger	gong	sung	
rang	prong	strung	
gang	strong	swung	
gangway	tongs	slung	
clang		sprung	
sprang			

LESSON 195: COMBINATION – N=NG (WORD BUILDING)

The instructor:

- Tells children that in the lesson words, *n* sound like *ng*.
- Points at the *n*, makes the associated *ng* sound, and asks children to repeat the sound.

For each word, the instructor:

- Displays the word, asks children to sound out the word, and allows children to decipher the word with minimal assistance.
- Recites the word aloud and directs children to:
  1. Build the word out of letter tiles.
  2. Point at each letter tile in the word while making the related sound.

n = ng

bank	thank	mink	chunk
blank	thanking	pink	trunk
clank	drank	sink	trunks
plank	sank	drink	stronger
rank	tank	think	hunger
Frank	ink	blink	hungry
Frank's	link	sunk	angry
crank			

LESSON 196: COMBINATION – ING AND DROPPING E PART 1 (WORD BUILDING)

The instructor:

- The instructor points at the *ing*, makes the associated sounds, and asks children to repeat the sounds.

- Tells children that changing some words to their *ing* form necessitates dropping the final e.
    1. hide – hiding
    2. close – closing

For each word, the instructor:

- Displays the word, asks children to sound out the word, and allows children to decipher the word with minimal assistance.

- Asks children to identify the related word ending in *e* (e.g. making – make)

- Recites the word aloud and directs children to:
    1. Build the word out of letter tiles.
    2. Point at each letter tile in the word while making the related sound.

Dropping e with ing

making	stoning	spading
grading	smoking	sloping
skating	hoping	closing
waving	curing	taking
hiding	wading	mining
riding	piling	storing
smiling	ranking	lining
chiming	draping	freezing
shining	raising	squeezing

LESSON 197: COMBINATION – ING AND DROPPING E PART 2 (WORD BUILDING)

The instructor:

- The instructor points at the *ing*, makes the associated sounds, and asks children to repeat the sounds.

- Tells children that changing some words to their *ing* form necessitates dropping the final e.
    1. please – pleasing
    2. tame – taming

For each word, the instructor:

- Displays the word, asks children to sound out the word, and allows children to decipher the word with minimal assistance.

- Asks children to identify the related word ending in *e* (e.g. filing – file)

- Recites the word aloud and directs children to:
    1. Build the word out of letter tiles.
    2. Point at each letter tile in the word while making the related sound.

Dropping e with ing

pleasing	framing	taming
leaving	blaming	siding
weaving	flaming	filing
praising	scraping	snoring
wasting	whining	hiring
pasting	bathing	driving
trading	thriving	blazing
striking	choking	tasting
stroking	chasing	shaving

LESSON 198: COMBINATIONS – KN=N AND GN=N (WORD BUILDING)

The instructor:

- Tells children that in the lesson words, *kn* sounds like *n*.
- Points at the *kn*, makes the associated *n* sound, and asks children to repeat the sound.
- Repeats the above instructions for *gn*.

For each word, the instructor:

- Displays the word, asks children to sound out the word, and allows children to decipher the word with minimal assistance.
- Recites the word aloud and directs children to:
    1. Build the word out of letter tiles.
    2. Point at each letter tile in the word while making the related sound.

kn = n

knob	known
knot	knight
knee	knead
kneel	kneads
knit	kneading
knits	knack
knife	knock
know	knocks
knows	knocking

gn = n

gnat
gnats
gnash
gnashes
sign
signboard

LESSON 199: COMBINATION – WR=R (WORD BUILDING)

The instructor:

- Tells children that in the lesson words, *wr* sounds like *r*.
- Points at the *wr*, makes the associated *r* sound, and asks children to repeat the sound.

For each word, the instructor:

- Displays the word, asks children to sound out the word, and allows children to decipher the word with minimal assistance.
- Recites the word aloud and directs children to:
    1. Build the word out of letter tiles.
    2. Point at each letter tile in the word while making the related sound.

wr = r

wrap	wrist
wraps	wrists
wren	wrong
wrench	write
wrenches	writes
wring	writing
wringer	wrote
wringing	wreck
wreath	wrecks

LESSON 200: COMBINATION – MB=M (WORD BUILDING)

The instructor:

- Tells children that in the lesson words, *mb* sounds like *m*.
- Points at the *mb*, makes the associated *m* sound, and asks children to repeat the sound.

For each word, the instructor:

- Displays the word, asks children to sound out the word, and allows children to decipher the word with minimal assistance.
- Recites the word aloud and directs children to:
  1. Build the word out of letter tiles.
  2. Point at each letter tile in the word while making the related sound.

mb = m

lamb	dumb
lambkin	crumb
limb	numb
comb	plumbing
climb	thumb

LESSON 201: COMBINATION – GU=G (WORD BUILDING)

The instructor:

- Tells children that in the lesson words, *gu* sounds like *g*.
- Points at the *gu*, makes the associated *g* sound, and asks children to repeat the sound.

For each word, the instructor:

- Displays the word, asks children to sound out the word, and allows children to decipher the word with minimal assistance.
- Recites the word aloud and directs children to:
  1. Build the word out of letter tiles.
  2. Point at each letter tile in the word while making the related sound.

gu = g

guess guest
guesses plague
Guy rogue
guide league
guides leagues
guiding

LESSON 202: COMBINATION – BU=B (WORD BUILDING)

The instructor:

- Tells children that in the lesson words, *bu* sounds like *b*.
- Points at the *bu*, makes the associated *b* sound, and asks children to repeat the sound.

For each word, the instructor:

- Displays the word, asks children to sound out the word, and allows children to decipher the word with minimal assistance.
- Recites the word aloud and directs children to:
    1. Build the word out of letter tiles.
    2. Point at each letter tile in the word while making the related sound.

bu = b

build	buy
builds	buys
builder	buyer
building	buying
built	

ELEMENTARY PHONICS

LESSON 203: COMBINATION – BT=T (WORD BUILDING)

The instructor:

- Tells children that in the lesson words, *bt* sounds like *t*.
- Points at the *bt*, makes the associated *t* sound, and asks children to repeat the sound.

For each word, the instructor:

- Displays the word, asks children to sound out the word, and allows children to decipher the word with minimal assistance.
- Recites the word aloud and directs children to:
  1. Build the word out of letter tiles.
  2. Point at each letter tile in the word while making the related sound.

bt = t

doubt **debt**
doubts **debts**
doubting

LESSON 204: MISCELLANEOUS – REVIEW (WORD BUILDING)

For each word, the instructor:

- Displays the word, asks children to sound out the word, and allows children to decipher the word with minimal assistance.
- Recites the word aloud and directs children to:
    1. Build the word out of letter tiles.
    2. Point at each letter tile in the word while making the related sound.

Review

wrist	wrench	doubt
comb	gnat	guest
guess	writes	wrong
build	know	knock
debts	guide	gnash
buy	kneel	dumb
wreath	limb	knot

LESSON 205: CONSONANTS AND VOWEL SOUNDS (WORD BUILDING)

The instructor:

- Tells children a vowel is short when there are two consonants between it and the next vowel, as in *h**o**lly*.
- Informs children a vowel is long when there is only one consonant between it and the next vowel, as in *h**o**ly*.

For each word, the instructor:

- Displays the word, asks children to sound out the word, and allows children to decipher the word with minimal assistance.
- Recites the word aloud and directs children to:
    1. Build the word out of letter tiles.
    2. Point at each letter tile in the word while making the related sound.

matting	pinning	holly
mating	pining	holy
lopping	dinner	latter
loping	diner	later
filling	mopping	hopping
filing	moping	hoping
slopping	shamming	batting
sloping	shaming	bating

LESSON 206: SAME SOUND DOUBLE CONSONANTS BETWEEN VOWELS (WORD BUILDING)

The instructor reminds children a vowel is short when there are two consonants between it and the next vowel, as in *happy*.

For each word, the instructor:

- Displays the word, asks children to sound out the word, and allows children to decipher the word with minimal assistance.
- Recites the word aloud and directs children to:
    1. Build the word out of letter tiles.
    2. Point at each letter tile in the word while making the related sound.

happy	planning	blotter
ladder	supper	cracker
bonnet	yellow	rabbit
motto	begging	carry
summer	shabby	hammer

LESSON 207: TWO OR MORE CONSONANTS BETWEEN VOWELS (WORD BUILDING)

The instructor reminds children a vowel is short when there are two consonants between it and the next vowel, as in *sister*.

For each word, the instructor:

- Displays the word, asks children to sound out the word, and allows children to decipher the word with minimal assistance.
- Recites the word aloud and directs children to:
  1. Build the word out of letter tiles.
  2. Point at each letter tile in the word while making the related sound.

napkin	velvet	public
silver	lifting	mending
pilgrim	pumpkin	pitcher
candy	sister	dentist
dustpan	renting	picnic
number	trumpet	melting
window	slender	empty
camping	crusty	thunder

LESSON 208: ONE CONSONANT BETWEEN VOWELS (WORD BUILDING)

The instructor reminds children a vowel is long when there is only one consonant between it and the next vowel, as in *zero*.

For each word, the instructor:

- Displays the word, asks children to sound out the word, and allows children to decipher the word with minimal assistance.
- Recites the word aloud and directs children to:
    1. Build the word out of letter tiles.
    2. Point at each letter tile in the word while making the related sound.

story	smiling	zero
closing	pupil	cozy
baker	pony	hero
duty	sober	tiger
navy	tulip	tiny
solo	lady	gravy
fever	clover	paper
music	shady	hazy

LESSON 209: COMBINATIONS – AI=SHORT I AND IE=LONG E (WORD BUILDING)

The instructor:

- Tells children that in the lesson words, *ai* sounds like *short i*.
- Points at the *ai*, makes the associated *short i* sound, and asks children to repeat the sound.
- Repeats the above instructions for the *long e* sound of *ie*.

For each word, the instructor:

- Displays the word, asks children to sound out the word, and allows children to decipher the word with minimal assistance.
- Recites the word aloud and directs children to:
    1. Build the word out of letter tiles.
    2. Point at each letter tile in the word while making the related sound.

ai = short i

mountain
fountain
captain

ie = long e

chief   tier
thief   wield
thieves   yield
brief   shield
field   grieve
priest   grieves

LESSON 210: COMBINATION – EA=LONG A (WORD BUILDING)

The instructor:

- Tells children that in the lesson words, *ea* sounds like *long a*.
- Points at the *ea*, makes the associated *long a* sound, and asks children to repeat the sound.

For each word, the instructor:

- Displays the word, asks children to sound out the word, and allows children to decipher the word with minimal assistance.
- Recites the word aloud and directs children to:
  1. Build the word out of letter tiles.
  2. Point at each letter tile in the word while making the related sound.

ea = long a

break	daybreak
breaks	great
breaker	greater
breakers	steak
breaking	beefsteak

LESSON 211: COMBINATION – EA=SHORT E (WORD BUILDING)

The instructor:

- Tells children that in the lesson words, *ea* sounds like *short e*.
- Points at the *ea*, makes the associated *short e* sound, and asks children to repeat the sound.

For each word, the instructor:

- Displays the word, asks children to sound out the word, and allows children to decipher the word with minimal assistance.
- Recites the word aloud and directs children to:
  1. Build the word out of letter tiles.
  2. Point at each letter tile in the word while making the related sound.

ea = short e

head	spread	heavy
dead	thread	sweat
read	deaf	breath
ready	meant	meadow
dread	health	feather
dreads	healthy	leather
lead	wealth	weather
bread	wealthy	

LESSON 212: COMBINATION – ED (WORD BUILDING)

The instructor points at the *ed*, makes the associated sound, and asks children to repeat the sound.

For each word, the instructor:

- Displays the word, asks children to sound out the word, and allows children to decipher the word with minimal assistance.
- Recites the word aloud and directs children to:
    1. Build the word out of letter tiles.
    2. Point at each letter tile in the word while making the related sound.

ed

petted	sifted	seated
landed	folded	pouted
faded	clouded	roasted
tested	boasted	handed
needed	tended	doubted
twisted	rented	coasted
wicked	jolted	mended
tinted	graded	weeded
crowded	waded	

LESSON 213: COMBINATION – ED=D (WORD BUILDING)

The instructor:

- Tells children that in the lesson words, *ed* sounds like *d*.
- Points at the *ed*, makes the associated *d* sound, and asks children to repeat the sound.

For each word, the instructor:

- Displays the word, asks children to sound out the word, and allows children to decipher the word with minimal assistance.
- Recites the word aloud and directs children to:
    1. Build the word out of letter tiles.
    2. Point at each letter tile in the word while making the related sound.

ed = d

sailed	frowned	buttered
played	foamed	roared
kneeled	crowed	wheeled
mired	breathed	scattered
plowed	pinned	shivered
aimed	prayed	cleaned
loaned	climbed	snowed
growled	sealed	canned
peeled	soured	

LESSON 214: COMBINATION – ED=T (WORD BUILDING)

The instructor:

- Tells children that in the lesson words, *ed* sounds like *t*.
- Points at the *ed*, makes the associated *t* sound, and asks children to repeat the sound.

For each word, the instructor:

- Displays the word, asks children to sound out the word, and allows children to decipher the word with minimal assistance.
- Recites the word aloud and directs children to:
    1. Build the word out of letter tiles.
    2. Point at each letter tile in the word while making the related sound.

ed = t

reached	liked	guessed
puffed	wrapped	dropped
baked	stamped	coaxed
clapped	leaped	checked
ticked	dressed	shipped
brushed	knocked	scraped
patched	wrenched	dashed
choked	packed	milked
wrecked	kissed	

LESSON 215: MISCELLANEOUS – REVIEW (WORD BUILDING)

For each word, the instructor:

- Displays the word, asks children to sound out the word, and allows children to decipher the word with minimal assistance.
- Recites the word aloud and directs children to:
    1. Build the word out of letter tiles.
    2. Point at each letter tile in the word while making the related sound.

Review

mounted	skated	sighed
battered	grunted	painted
rusted	wretched	lacked
cried	begged	mailed
floated	ailed	kicked
pained	mixed	rained
strayed	tacked	heaped
cracked	missed	lighted

LESSON 216: COMBINATIONS – IE/EY=LONG E (WORD BUILDING)

The instructor:

- Tells children that in the lesson words, *ie* sounds like *long e*.
- Points at the *ie*, makes the associated *long e* sound, and asks children to repeat the sound.
- Repeats the above instructions for the *long e* sound of *ey* as in *valley*.

For each word, the instructor:

- Displays the word, asks children to sound out the word, and allows children to decipher the word with minimal assistance.
- Recites the word aloud and directs children to:
    1. Build the word out of letter tiles.
    2. Point at each letter tile in the word while making the related sound.

ie/ey = long e

Annie	stories	carries
Jimmie	candies	berries
Bessie	cities	copies
Hattie	ladies	pansies
Jessie	pennies	donkey
Lizzie	empties	chimney
Nellie	fifties	alley
Willie	puppies	valley
kitties	sixties	pulley
daisies		

LESSON 217: COMBINATIONS – EI/EIGH/EY=LONG A (WORD BUILDING)

The instructor:

- Tells children that in lesson words, *ei* sounds like *long a*.
- Points at the *ei*, makes the associated *long a* sound, and asks children to repeat the sound.
- Repeats the above instructions for the *long a* sounds of *eigh* and *ey*.

For each word, the instructor:

- Displays the word, asks children to sound out the word, and allows children to decipher the word with minimal assistance.
- Recites the word aloud and directs children to:
    1. Build the word out of letter tiles.
    2. Point at each letter tile in the word while making the related sound.

ei/eigh/ey = long a

skein	eighteen	sleigh
reins	eighty	neigh
reindeer	eighty-five	freight
veil	eighty-six	they
vein	eighty-eight	whey
reign	weigh	prey
eight	weight	greyhound

LESSON 218: COMBINATION – LONG OO (WORD BUILDING)

The instructor demonstrates the *long oo* sound (as in *room*) and asks children to repeat the sound.

For each word, the instructor:

- Displays the word, asks children to sound out the word, and allows children to decipher the word with minimal assistance.

- Recites the word aloud and directs children to:
    1. Build the word out of letter tiles.
    2. Point at each letter tile in the word while making the related sound.

long oo

boot	room	looped	soothe
too	boom	droop	boost
hoof	bloom	troop	choose
roof	gloom	stoop	coo
proof	gloomy	hoop	coop
cool	soon	goose	scoop
pool	moon	loose	groove
tool	noon	broom	poor
stool	spoon	root	smooth
spool	teaspoon	hoot	smoothed
food	loop	shoot	tooth

LESSON 219: COMBINATION – O=LONG OO (WORD BUILDING)

The instructor:

- Tells children that in the lesson words, *o* sounds like *long oo*.
- Points at the *o*, makes the associated *long oo* sound, and asks children to repeat the sound.

For each word, the instructor:

- Displays the word, asks children to sound out the word, and allows children to decipher the word with minimal assistance.
- Recites the word aloud and directs children to:
  1. Build the word out of letter tiles.
  2. Point at each letter tile in the word while making the related sound.

o = long oo

do	move
to	shoe
prove	shoemaker
proves	tomb

LESSON 220: COMBINATION – U=LONG OO (WORD BUILDING)

The instructor:

- Tells children that in the lesson words, *u* sounds like *long oo*.
- Points at the *u*, makes the associated *long oo* sound, and asks children to repeat the sound.

For each word, the instructor:

- Displays the word, asks children to sound out the word, and allows children to decipher the word with minimal assistance.
- Recites the word aloud and directs children to:
  1. Build the word out of letter tiles.
  2. Point at each letter tile in the word while making the related sound.

u = long oo

blue	rule
glue	prune
true	truth
rude	Ruth
ruby	Gertrude
rubies	

LESSON 221: COMBINATION – OU=LONG OO (WORD BUILDING)

The instructor:

- Tells children that in the lesson words, *ou* sounds like *long oo*.
- Points at the *ou*, makes the associated *long oo* sound, and asks children to repeat the sound.

For each word, the instructor:

- Displays the word, asks children to sound out the word, and allows children to decipher the word with minimal assistance.
- Recites the word aloud and directs children to:
    1. Build the word out of letter tiles.
    2. Point at each letter tile in the word while making the related sound.

ou = long oo

soup
croup
group
grouped

LESSON 222: COMBINATION – UI=LONG OO (WORD BUILDING)

The instructor:

- Tells children that in the lesson words, *ui* sounds like *long oo*.
- Points at the *ui*, makes the associated *long oo* sound, and asks children to repeat the sound.

For each word, the instructor:

- Displays the word, asks children to sound out the word, and allows children to decipher the word with minimal assistance.
- Recites the word aloud and directs children to:
    1. Build the word out of letter tiles.
    2. Point at each letter tile in the word while making the related sound.

ui = long oo

suit

fruit

bruise

bruised

cruise

LESSON 223: COMBINATION – EW=LONG OO (WORD BUILDING)

The instructor:

- Tells children that in the lesson words, *ew* sounds like *long oo*.
- Points at the *ew*, makes the associated *long oo* sound, and asks children to repeat the sound.

For each word, the instructor:

- Displays the word, asks children to sound out the word, and allows children to decipher the word with minimal assistance.
- Recites the word aloud and directs children to:
  1. Build the word out of letter tiles.
  2. Point at each letter tile in the word while making the related sound.

ew = long oo

drew	strew
grew	threw
crew	chew
screw	flew

LESSON 224: COMBINATION – WH=H (WORD BUILDING)

The instructor:

- Tells children that in the lesson words, *wh* sounds like *h*.
- Points at the *wh*, makes the associated *h* sound, and asks children to repeat the sound.

For each word, the instructor:

- Displays the word, asks children to sound out the word, and allows children to decipher the word with minimal assistance.
- Recites the word aloud and directs children to:
    1. Build the word out of letter tiles.
    2. Point at each letter tile in the word while making the related sound.

wh = h

who

whom

whose

LESSON 225: COMBINATION – EW=LONG U (WORD BUILDING)

The instructor:

- Tells children that in the lesson words, *ew* sounds like *long u*.
- Points at the *ew*, makes the associated *long u* sound, and asks children to repeat the sound.

For each word, the instructor:

- Displays the word, asks children to sound out the word, and allows children to decipher the word with minimal assistance.
- Recites the word aloud and directs children to:
    1. Build the word out of letter tiles.
    2. Point at each letter tile in the word while making the related sound.

ew = long u

mew
new
dew
stew
few

LESSON 226: COMBINATION – OO=LONG O (WORD BUILDING)

The instructor:

- Tells children that in the lesson words, *oo* sounds like *long o*.
- Points at the *oo*, makes the associated *long o* sound, and asks children to repeat the sound.

For each word, the instructor:

- Displays the word, asks children to sound out the word, and allows children to decipher the word with minimal assistance.
- Recites the word aloud and directs children to:
    1. Build the word out of letter tiles.
    2. Point at each letter tile in the word while making the related sound.

oo = long o

door

floor

LESSON 227: COMBINATION – SHORT OO (WORD BUILDING)

The instructor points at the *oo*, makes the associated *short oo* sound (as in *look*), and asks children to repeat the sound.

For each word, the instructor:

- Displays the word, asks children to sound out the word, and allows children to decipher the word with minimal assistance.
- Recites the word aloud and directs children to:
    1. Build the word out of letter tiles.
    2. Point at each letter tile in the word while making the related sound.

short oo

good	woodshed	look
goodbye	cook	looked
hood	cooking	brook
childhood	hook	brooks
stood	fishhook	crook
understood	shook	crooked
wood	took	foot
woods	undertook	wool
woodpile		

LESSON 228: COMBINATIONS – O/OUL=SHORT OO (WORD BUILDING)

The instructor:

- Tells children that in the lesson words, *o* sounds like *short oo*.
- Points at the *o*, makes the associated *short oo* sound, and asks children to repeat the sound.
- Repeats the above instructions for the *short oo* sound of *oul*.

For each word, the instructor:

- Displays the word, asks children to sound out the word, and allows children to decipher the word with minimal assistance.
- Recites the word aloud and directs children to:
    1. Build the word out of letter tiles.
    2. Point at each letter tile in the word while making the related sound.

o = short oo   oul = short oo

wolf   could
wolves   would
                  should

LESSON 229: COMBINATION – U=SHORT OO (WORD BUILDING)

The instructor:

- Tells children that in the lesson words, *u* sounds like *short oo*.
- Points at the *u*, makes the associated *short oo* sound, and asks children to repeat the sound.

For each word, the instructor:

- Displays the word, asks children to sound out the word, and allows children to decipher the word with minimal assistance.
- Recites the word aloud and directs children to:
    1. Build the word out of letter tiles.
    2. Point at each letter tile in the word while making the related sound.

u = short oo

put	bushes	pull
putting	cuckoo	pulling
puss	butcher	pulled
push	pudding	pulpit
bush	puddings	full

LESSON 230: COMBINATION – FUL (WORD BUILDING)

The instructor points at the combination, *ful*, makes the associated sounds, and asks children to repeat the sounds.

For each word, the instructor:

- Displays the word, asks children to sound out the word, and allows children to decipher the word with minimal assistance.

- Recites the word aloud and directs children to:
    1. Build the word out of letter tiles.
    2. Point at each letter tile in the word while making the related sound.

ful

cheerful	truthful	playful
thankful	painful	plentiful
dreadful	fretful	healthful
joyful	frightful	restful
tearful	fearful	useful
spiteful	bashful	hopeful
helpful	hateful	shameful
doubtful	grateful	

LESSON 231: COMBINATION – OY (WORD BUILDING)

The instructor points at the *oy*, makes the associated sound, and asks children to repeat the sound.

For each word, the instructor:

- Displays the word, asks children to sound out the word, and allows children to decipher the word with minimal assistance.
- Recites the word aloud and directs children to:
  1. Build the word out of letter tiles.
  2. Point at each letter tile in the word while making the related sound.

oy

toy	boyhood
Roy	enjoy
joy	joyful
soy	oyster

LESSON 232: COMBINATION – OI=OY (WORD BUILDING)

The instructor:

- Tells children that in the lesson words, *oi* sounds like *oy*.
- Points at the *oi*, makes the associated *oy* sound, and asks children to repeat the sound.

For each word, the instructor:

- Displays the word, asks children to sound out the word, and allows children to decipher the word with minimal assistance.
- Recites the word aloud and directs children to:
    1. Build the word out of letter tiles.
    2. Point at each letter tile in the word while making the related sound.

oi = oy

oil	joint
toil	point
boil	moist
spoil	noise
coin	noisy
join	

ELEMENTARY PHONICS

LESSON 233: COMBINATION – LE PART 1 (WORD BUILDING)

The instructor points at the *le*, makes the associated sound, and asks children to repeat the sound.

For each word, the instructor:

- Displays the word, asks children to sound out the word, and allows children to decipher the word with minimal assistance.
- Recites the word aloud and directs children to:
  1. Build the word out of letter tiles.
  2. Point at each letter tile in the word while making the related sound.

le

apple	cuddle	bottle
cattle	puddle	beetle
saddle	tinkle	cradle
tumble	pickle	wiggle
candle	tangle	handle
thimble	kettle	eagle
steeple	maple	tremble

LESSON 234: COMBINATION – LE PART 2 (WORD BUILDING)

The instructor points at the *le*, makes the associated sound, and asks children to repeat the sound.

For each word, the instructor:

- Displays the word, asks children to sound out the word, and allows children to decipher the word with minimal assistance.
- Recites the word aloud and directs children to:
    1. Build the word out of letter tiles.
    2. Point at each letter tile in the word while making the related sound.

le

bundle	rumble	buckle
brittle	single	paddle
middle	dimple	twinkle
people	bugle	wrinkle
table	needle	pebble
ruffle	stable	settle
crackle	riddle	crumble
stumble	battle	shingle

LESSON 235: COMBINATION – TLE=LE (WORD BUILDING)

The instructor:

- Tells children that in the lesson words, *tle* sounds like *le*.
- Points at the *tle*, makes the associated *le* sound, and asks children to repeat the sound.

For each word, the instructor:

- Displays the word, asks children to sound out the word, and allows children to decipher the word with minimal assistance.
- Recites the word aloud and directs children to:
    1. Build the word out of letter tiles.
    2. Point at each letter tile in the word while making the related sound.

tle = le

whistle   nestle
thistle   rustle
bristle   trestle
wrestle

LESSON 236: C=S BEFORE E/I/Y (WORD BUILDING)

The instructor:

- Tells children that in the lesson words, *c* sounds like *s*, especially when followed by *e*, *i*, or *y*.
- Points at the *c*, makes the associated *s* sound, and asks children to repeat the sound.

For each word, the instructor:

- Displays the word, asks children to sound out the word, and allows children to decipher the word with minimal assistance.
- Ask children which letter follows the *c* that sounds like *s*.
- Recites the word aloud and directs children to:
    1. Build the word out of letter tiles.
    2. Point at each letter tile in the word while making the related sound.

c = s before e/i/y

ice	trace	cell	city
rice	brace	center	cider
mice	Grace	cease	cinders
nice	fence	piece	icicle
slice	quince	niece	juice
price	since	fierce	juicy
twice	Prince	voice	spice
face	Alice	choice	spicy
lace	ounce	grocery	cyclone
place	bounce	ceil	bicycle
space	flounce	pencil	Lucy
race			

LESSON 237: G=J BEFORE E/I/J (WORD BUILDING)

The instructor:

- Tells children that in the lesson words, *g* sounds like *j*, especially when followed by *e*, *i*, or *y*.
- Points at the *g*, makes the associated *j* sound, and asks children to repeat the sound.

For each word, the instructor:

- Displays the word, asks children to sound out the word, and allows children to decipher the word with minimal assistance.
- Ask children which letter follows the *g* that sounds like *j*.
- Recites the word aloud and directs children to:
    1. Build the word out of letter tiles.
    2. Point at each letter tile in the word while making the related sound.

g = j before e/i/y

gem	range	fringe	ginger
age	change	plunge	gingerbread
gage	strange	Roger	magic
sage	stranger	gentle	Gyp
rage	danger	huge	Egypt
stage	manger	college	gypsy
cage	hinge	engine	dingy
page			

LESSON 238: COMBINATION – DG=J (WORD BUILDING)

The instructor:

- Tells children that in the lesson words, *dg* sounds like *j*.
- Points at the *dg*, makes the associated *j* sound, and asks children to repeat the sound.

For each word, the instructor:

- Displays the word, asks children to sound out the word, and allows children to decipher the word with minimal assistance.
- Recites the word aloud and directs children to:
  1. Build the word out of letter tiles.
  2. Point at each letter tile in the word while making the related sound.

dg = j

badge	sledge	dodge
Madge	pledge	lodge
edge	dredge	budge
ledge	ridge	nudge
hedge	bridge	judge
wedge		

ELEMENTARY PHONICS

LESSON 239: COMBINATION – LY (WORD BUILDING)

The instructor points at the *ly*, makes the associated sound, and asks children to repeat the sound.

For each word, the instructor:

- Displays the word, asks children to sound out the word, and allows children to decipher the word with minimal assistance.
- Recites the word aloud and directs children to:
  1. Build the word out of letter tiles.
  2. Point at each letter tile in the word while making the related sound.

ly

safely	loudly	badly	lately
gaily	kingly	freely	truly
fully	boldly	swiftly	bravely
sadly	slyly	quickly	neatly
gladly	nicely	lonely	nearly
lightly	softly	mostly	wholly
slowly	likely	gently	closely
poorly	daily	kindly	ugly

LESSON 240: COMBINATION – LESS (WORD BUILDING)

The instructor points at the *less*, makes the associated sound, and asks children to repeat the sound.

For each word, the instructor:

- Displays the word, asks children to sound out the word, and allows children to decipher the word with minimal assistance.
- Recites the word aloud and directs children to:
  1. Build the word out of letter tiles.
  2. Point at each letter tile in the word while making the related sound.

less

less	tasteless	shameless
blameless	tireless	priceless
aimless	lifeless	endless
wireless	painless	senseless
useless	hopeless	thankless
homeless	boundless	restless
fearless	matchless	speechless

ELEMENTARY PHONICS

LESSON 241: COMBINATION – NESS (WORD BUILDING)

The instructor points at the *ness*, makes the associated sound, and asks children to repeat the sound.

For each word, the instructor:

- Displays the word, asks children to sound out the word, and allows children to decipher the word with minimal assistance.
- Recites the word aloud and directs children to:
    1. Build the word out of letter tiles.
    2. Point at each letter tile in the word while making the related sound.

ness

sweetness	lameness	sadness
meanness	thickness	sickness
kindness	weakness	goodness
illness	loneliness	happiness
stillness	soreness	

LESSON 242: COMBINATION – EST (WORD BUILDING)

The instructor points at the *est*, makes the associated sound, and asks children to repeat the sound.

For each word, the instructor:

- Displays the word, asks children to sound out the word, and allows children to decipher the word with minimal assistance.

- Recites the word aloud and directs children to:
    1. Build the word out of letter tiles.
    2. Point at each letter tile in the word while making the related sound.

est

coldest	wildest	oldest	grandest
nicest	sweetest	widest	biggest
loudest	lamest	dearest	nearest
lightest	dampest	brightest	blackest
slowest	sorest	roundest	newest
kindest	stiffest	reddest	stillest
tamest	wisest	softest	thickest
safest	latest	crossest	freshest
tightest	finest	gladdest	happiest
ripest	lowest		

LESSON 243: COMBINATION – ER (WORD BUILDING)

The instructor points at the *er*, makes the associated sound, and asks children to repeat the sound.

For each word, the instructor:

- Displays the word, asks children to sound out the word, and allows children to decipher the word with minimal assistance.
- Recites the word aloud and directs children to:
  1. Build the word out of letter tiles.
  2. Point at each letter tile in the word while making the related sound.

er

lantern
desert
finger
rooster
every
flutter
spider

LESSON 244: COMBINATION – AR=ER (WORD BUILDING)

The instructor:

- Tells children that in the lesson words, *ar* sounds like *er*.
- Points at the *ar*, makes the associated *er* sound, and asks children to repeat the sound.

For each word, the instructor:

- Displays the word, asks children to sound out the word, and allows children to decipher the word with minimal assistance.
- Recites the word aloud and directs children to:
    1. Build the word out of letter tiles.
    2. Point at each letter tile in the word while making the related sound.

ar = er

backward

beggar

cedar

dollar

LESSON 245: COMBINATION – EAR=ER (WORD BUILDING)

The instructor:

- Tells children that in the lesson words, *ear* sounds like *er*.
- Points at the *ear*, makes the associated *er* sound, and asks children to repeat the sound.

For each word, the instructor:

- Displays the word, asks children to sound out the word, and allows children to decipher the word with minimal assistance.
- Recites the word aloud and directs children to:
    1. Build the word out of letter tiles.
    2. Point at each letter tile in the word while making the related sound.

ear = er

earn
learn
search
earth
heard
pearl

LESSON 246: COMBINATION – IR=ER (WORD BUILDING)

The instructor:

- Tells children that in the lesson words, *ir* sounds like *er*.
- Points at the *ir*, makes the associated *er* sound, and asks children to repeat the sound.

For each word, the instructor:

- Displays the word, asks children to sound out the word, and allows children to decipher the word with minimal assistance.
- Recites the word aloud and directs children to:
    1. Build the word out of letter tiles.
    2. Point at each letter tile in the word while making the related sound.

ir = er

bird	birthday
chirp	firm
girl	squirm
first	third
skirt	whirl
shirt	squirrel
stir	thirty
dirt	circle
fir	thirsty

LESSON 247: COMBINATION – OR=ER (WORD BUILDING)

The instructor:

- Tells children that in the lesson words, *or* sounds like *er*.
- Points at the *or*, makes the associated *er* sound, and asks children to repeat the sound.

For each word, the instructor:

- Displays the word, asks children to sound out the word, and allows children to decipher the word with minimal assistance.
- Recites the word aloud and directs children to:
  1. Build the word out of letter tiles.
  2. Point at each letter tile in the word while making the related sound.

or = er

word	stubborn
work	flavor
world	tailor
worm	sailor
worse	doctor
worst	neighbor
worth	

LESSON 248: COMBINATION – UR=ER (WORD BUILDING)

The instructor:

- Tells children that in the lesson words, *ur* sounds like *er*.
- Points at the *ur*, makes the associated *er* sound, and asks children to repeat the sound.

For each word, the instructor:

- Displays the word, asks children to sound out the word, and allows children to decipher the word with minimal assistance.
- Recites the word aloud and directs children to:
  1. Build the word out of letter tiles.
  2. Point at each letter tile in the word while making the related sound.

ur = er

bur	hurl	curve
fur	purse	burst
blur	nurse	purple
sturdy	churn	church
urge	burn	turtle
curl	turn	further
curly	hurt	nursery

ELEMENTARY PHONICS

LESSON 249: COMBINATION – ISH (WORD BUILDING)

The instructor points at the *ish*, makes the associated sound, and asks children to repeat the sound.

For each word, the instructor:

- Displays the word, asks children to sound out the word, and allows children to decipher the word with minimal assistance.
- Recites the word aloud and directs children to:
    1. Build the word out of letter tiles.
    2. Point at each letter tile in the word while making the related sound.

ish

dish	finish	Irish
wish	polish	Spanish
fish	selfish	British
rubbish	punish	furnish
foolish	stylish	

LESSON 250: MISCELLANEOUS – REVIEW (WORD BUILDING)

For each word, the instructor:

- Displays the word, asks children to sound out the word, and allows children to decipher the word with minimal assistance.
- Recites the word aloud and directs children to:
    1. Build the word out of letter tiles.
    2. Point at each letter tile in the word while making the related sound.

Review

butterfly	sunbeams	himself
grapevine	sunset	firefly
raindrops	sunrise	fireside
rainbow	cobweb	midnight
dewdrops	forget	windmill
sunshine	blackboard	daylight

ELEMENTARY PHONICS

LESSON 251: COMBINATION – A LIKE ST(A)R PART 1 (WORD BUILDING)

The instructor:

- Tells children that in the lesson words, *a* sounds like *a* in *st(a)r*.
- Points at the *a*, makes the associated *a* sound as in *star*, and asks children to repeat the sound.

For each word, the instructor:

- Displays the word, asks children to sound out the word, and allows children to decipher the word with minimal assistance.
- Recites the word aloud and directs children to:
  1. Build the word out of letter tiles.
  2. Point at each letter tile in the word while making the related sound.

$$a = st(a)r$$

bar	jar	bark	lark
marble	tar	dark	arm
march	star	darkness	farm
arch	starlight	mark	harm
car	starch	park	harmless
card	starve	parlor	charm
scar	hard	spark	
far	yard	sparkle	

LESSON 252: COMBINATION – A LIKE ST(A)R PART 2 (WORD BUILDING)

The instructor:

- Tells children that in the lesson words, *a* sounds like *a* in *st(a)r*.
- Points at the *a*, makes the associated *a* sound as in *star*, and asks children to repeat the sound.

For each word, the instructor:

- Displays the word, asks children to sound out the word, and allows children to decipher the word with minimal assistance.
- Recites the word aloud and directs children to:
  1. Build the word out of letter tiles.
  2. Point at each letter tile in the word while making the related sound.

a = st(a)r

barn	dart	charge
darn	part	sharp
yarn	party	harvest
art	chart	grandpa
artist	start	grandma
tart	startle	father
cart	large	grandfather

LESSON 253: COMBINATION – AU LIKE ST(A)R (WORD BUILDING)

The instructor:

- Tells children that in the lesson words, *au* sounds like *a* in *st(a)r*.
- Points at the *au*, makes the associated *a* sound as in *aunt*, and asks children to repeat the sound.

For each word, the instructor:

- Displays the word, asks children to sound out the word, and allows children to decipher the word with minimal assistance.
- Recites the word aloud and directs children to:
    1. Build the word out of letter tiles.
    2. Point at each letter tile in the word while making the related sound.

au = st(a)r

aunt
jaunt
launch
craunch
laundry

LESSON 254: COMBINATIONS – LF=F AND LV=V (WORD BUILDING)

The instructor:

- Tells children that in the lesson words, *lf* sounds like *f*.
- Points at the *lf*, makes the associated *f* sound, and asks children to repeat the sound.
- Repeats the above instructions for *lv*.

For each word, the instructor:

- Displays the word, asks children to sound out the word, and allows children to decipher the word with minimal assistance.
- Recites the word aloud and directs children to:
    1. Build the word out of letter tiles.
    2. Point at each letter tile in the word while making the related sound.

lf = f   lv = v

calf   calves
half   halves

ELEMENTARY PHONICS

LESSON 255: COMBINATION – AIR (WORD BUILDING)

The instructor points at the *air*, makes the associated sound, and asks children to repeat the sound.

For each word, the instructor:

- Displays the word, asks children to sound out the word, and allows children to decipher the word with minimal assistance.
- Recites the word aloud and directs children to:
    1. Build the word out of letter tiles.
    2. Point at each letter tile in the word while making the related sound.

air

air	hairbrush
airy	pair
fair	armchair
fairy	stair
fairest	staircase
hair	stairway

LESSON 256: COMBINATION – AR=AIR (WORD BUILDING)

The instructor:

- Tells children that in the lesson words, *ar* sounds like *air*.
- Points at the *ar*, makes the associated *air* sound, and asks children to repeat the sound.

For each word, the instructor:

- Displays the word, asks children to sound out the word, and allows children to decipher the word with minimal assistance.
- Recites the word aloud and directs children to:
  1. Build the word out of letter tiles.
  2. Point at each letter tile in the word while making the related sound.

ar = air

care	barefoot	glare
careful	threadbare	glaring
carefully	hare	flare
careless	spare	snare
carelessly	square	stare
carelessness	squarely	share
careworn	rare	shared
dare	rarely	scare
daring	rarest	scarecrow
fare	ware	scarce
farewell	hardware	scarcely
bare		

LESSON 257: COMBINATION – EAR=AIR (WORD BUILDING)

The instructor:

- Tells children that in the lesson words, *ear* sounds like *air*.
- Points at the *ear*, makes the associated *air* sound, and asks children to repeat the sound.

For each word, the instructor:

- Displays the word, asks children to sound out the word, and allows children to decipher the word with minimal assistance.
- Recites the word aloud and directs children to:
    1. Build the word out of letter tiles.
    2. Point at each letter tile in the word while making the related sound.

ear = air

tear	bear
tearing	grizzly bear
wear	polar bear
wears	pear

LESSON 258: COMBINATION – ERE=AIR (WORD BUILDING)

The instructor:

- Tells children that in the lesson words, *ere* sounds like *air*.
- Points at the *ere*, makes the associated *air* sound, and asks children to repeat the sound.

For each word, the instructor:

- Displays the word, asks children to sound out the word, and allows children to decipher the word with minimal assistance.
- Recites the word aloud and directs children to:
    1. Build the word out of letter tiles.
    2. Point at each letter tile in the word while making the related sound.

ere = air

ere wherever
there nowhere
therefore elsewhere
where

LESSON 259: COMBINATION – EIR=AIR (WORD BUILDING)

The instructor:

- Tells children that in the lesson words, *eir* sounds like *air*.
- Points at the *eir*, makes the associated *air* sound, and asks children to repeat the sound.

For each word, the instructor:

- Displays the word, asks children to sound out the word, and allows children to decipher the word with minimal assistance.
- Recites the word aloud and directs children to:
  1. Build the word out of letter tiles.
  2. Point at each letter tile in the word while making the related sound.

eir = air

heir

heirs

their

theirs

LESSON 260: COMBINATION – AW (WORD BUILDING)

The instructor points at the *aw*, makes the associated sound, and asks children to repeat the sound.

For each word, the instructor:

- Displays the word, asks children to sound out the word, and allows children to decipher the word with minimal assistance.
- Recites the word aloud and directs children to:
  1. Build the word out of letter tiles.
  2. Point at each letter tile in the word while making the related sound.

aw

jaw	draw	strawberry
gnaw	thaw	awning
law	awl	shawl
claw	scrawl	dawn
paw	squaw	lawn
hawk	straw	yawn

LESSON 261: COMBINATION – A=AW (WORD BUILDING)

The instructor:

- Tells children that in the lesson words, *a* sounds like *aw*.
- Points at the *a*, makes the associated *aw* sound, and asks children to repeat the sound.

For each word, the instructor:

- Displays the word, asks children to sound out the word, and allows children to decipher the word with minimal assistance.
- Recites the word aloud and directs children to:
    1. Build the word out of letter tiles.
    2. Point at each letter tile in the word while making the related sound.

a = aw

all	tall	sidewalk
almost	wall	talk
ball	walnut	chalk
baseball	stall	stalk
call	small	wigwam
fall	salt	water
hall	walk	want

LESSON 262: COMBINATION – AU=AW (WORD BUILDING)

The instructor:

- Tells children that in the lesson words, *au* sounds like *aw*.
- Points at the *au*, makes the associated *aw* sound, and asks children to repeat the sound.

For each word, the instructor:

- Displays the word, asks children to sound out the word, and allows children to decipher the word with minimal assistance.
- Recites the word aloud and directs children to:
    1. Build the word out of letter tiles.
    2. Point at each letter tile in the word while making the related sound.

au = aw

fault   pause
saucer   haul
cause   author
gauze   Paul

LESSON 263: COMBINATION – AUGH=AW (WORD BUILDING)

The instructor:

- Tells children that in the lesson words, *augh* sounds like *aw*.
- Points at the *augh*, makes the associated *aw* sound, and asks children to repeat the sound.

For each word, the instructor:

- Displays the word, asks children to sound out the word, and allows children to decipher the word with minimal assistance.
- Recites the word aloud and directs children to:
    1. Build the word out of letter tiles.
    2. Point at each letter tile in the word while making the related sound.

augh = aw

caught

taught

naught

distraught

LESSON 264: COMBINATION – OUGH=AW (WORD BUILDING)

The instructor:

- Tells children that in the lesson words, *ough* sounds like *aw*.
- Points at the *ough*, makes the associated *aw* sound, and asks children to repeat the sound.

For each word, the instructor:

- Displays the word, asks children to sound out the word, and allows children to decipher the word with minimal assistance.
- Recites the word aloud and directs children to:
    1. Build the word out of letter tiles.
    2. Point at each letter tile in the word while making the related sound.

ough = aw

ought   sought
bought   thought
brought   nought
fought

LESSON 265: COMBINATION – OUGH=LONG O (WORD BUILDING)

The instructor:

- Tells children that in the lesson words, *ough* sounds like *long o*.
- Points at the *ough*, makes the associated sound, and asks children to repeat the sound.

For each word, the instructor:

- Displays the word, asks children to sound out the word, and allows children to decipher the word with minimal assistance.
- Recites the word aloud and directs children to:
    1. Build the word out of letter tiles.
    2. Point at each letter tile in the word while making the related sound.

ough = long o

though
although
dough
doughnut
borough

LESSON 266: COMBINATION – A LIKE B(A)SKET (WORD BUILDING)

The instructor:

- Tells children that in the lesson words, *a* sounds like the *a* in *b(a)sket*.
- Points at the *a*, makes the associated sound, and asks children to repeat the sound.

For each word, the instructor:

- Displays the word, asks children to sound out the word, and allows children to decipher the word with minimal assistance.
- Recites the word aloud and directs children to:
    1. Build the word out of letter tiles.
    2. Point at each letter tile in the word while making the related sound.

a = b(a)sket

ant	craft	cast	glass
grant	after	fast	grass
slant	afterward	last	mass
chance	rafter	blast	pass
dance	ask	mast	chaff
glance	task	master	giraffe
France	mask	past	branch
raft	clasp	path	brass
draft	grasp	bath	class

LESSON 267: COMBINATION – A=SHORT O (WORD BUILDING)

The instructor:

- Tells children that in the lesson words, *a* sounds like *short o*.
- Points at the *a*, makes the associated *short o* sound, and asks children to repeat the sound.

For each word, the instructor:

- Displays the word, asks children to sound out the word, and allows children to decipher the word with minimal assistance.
- Recites the word aloud and directs children to:
  1. Build the word out of letter tiles.
  2. Point at each letter tile in the word while making the related sound.

a = short o

swan	wash	waffles
wand	washing	wallow
wander	washboard	swallow
wanderer	washtub	swallows
wandering	whitewash	swamp
wasp	squash	swamps
wasps	wad	swampy
watch	wads	quality
watchman	waffle	quantity
watchful		

LESSON 268: COMBINATION – O=SHORT U PART 1 (WORD BUILDING)

The instructor:

- Tells children that in the lesson words, *o* sounds like *short u*.
- Points at the *o*, makes the associated *short u* sound, and asks children to repeat the sound.

For each word, the instructor:

- Displays the word, asks children to sound out the word, and allows children to decipher the word with minimal assistance.
- Recites the word aloud and directs children to:
    1. Build the word out of letter tiles.
    2. Point at each letter tile in the word while making the related sound.

o = short u

son	some	come
grandson	sometime	coming
ton	sometimes	love
won	somewhat	lovely
wonder	somewhere	loveliest
wonderful	somebody	above
wonderfully	somebody's	shove
none	somehow	dove
done	something	gloves

LESSON 269: COMBINATION – O=SHORT U PART 2 (WORD BUILDING)

The instructor:

- Tells children that in the lesson words, *o* sounds like *short u*.
- Points at the *o*, makes the associated *short u* sound, and asks children to repeat the sound.

For each word, the instructor:

- Displays the word, asks children to sound out the word, and allows children to decipher the word with minimal assistance.
- Recites the word aloud and directs children to:
    1. Build the word out of letter tiles.
    2. Point at each letter tile in the word while making the related sound.

o = short u

sponge	color	mother
sponges	colors	mother's
tongue	colored	grandmother
tongues	comfort	brother
front	other	smother
month	others	smothered
nothing	another	dozen
cover	govern	London
covered		

LESSON 270: COMBINATION – OU=SHORT U (WORD BUILDING)

The instructor:

- Tells children that in the lesson words, *ou* sounds like *short u*.
- Points at the *ou*, makes the associated *short u* sound, and asks children to repeat the sound.

For each word, the instructor:

- Displays the word, asks children to sound out the word, and allows children to decipher the word with minimal assistance.
- Recites the word aloud and directs children to:
  1. Build the word out of letter tiles.
  2. Point at each letter tile in the word while making the related sound.

ou = short u

young
younger
wondrous
serious
touched
trouble

southern
double
country
countries
couple

LESSON 271: COMBINATION – OO=SHORT U (WORD BUILDING)

The instructor:

- Tells children that in the lesson words, *oo* sounds like *short u*.
- Points at the *oo*, makes the associated *short u* sound, and asks children to repeat the sound.

For each word, the instructor:

- Displays the word, asks children to sound out the word, and allows children to decipher the word with minimal assistance.
- Recites the word aloud and directs children to:
    1. Build the word out of letter tiles.
    2. Point at each letter tile in the word while making the related sound.

oo = short u

flood   blood
flooded   bloody
flooding

LESSON 272: OBSCURE A – PART 1 (WORD BUILDING)

The instructor:

- Tells children that in the lesson words, *a* sounds like *obscure a* and is pronounced as *uh*.
- Points at the *a*, makes the associated *obscure a* (*uh*) sound, and asks children to repeat the sound.

For each word, the instructor:

- Displays the word, asks children to sound out the word, and allows children to decipher the word with minimal assistance.
- Recites the word aloud and directs children to:
    1. Build the word out of letter tiles.
    2. Point at each letter tile in the word while making the related sound.

obscure a

ago	alike	arise
awoke	afraid	along
adrift	around	soda
afloat	away	sofa
amid	astray	Clara
alone	about	India
asleep	aloud	

LESSON 273: OBSCURE A – PART 2 (WORD BUILDING)

The instructor:

- Tells children that in the lesson words, *a* sounds like *obscure a* and is pronounced as *uh*.
- Points at the *a*, makes the associated *obscure a* (*uh*) sound, and asks children to repeat the sound.

For each word, the instructor:

- Displays the word, asks children to sound out the word, and allows children to decipher the word with minimal assistance.
- Recites the word aloud and directs children to:
    1. Build the word out of letter tiles.
    2. Point at each letter tile in the word while making the related sound.

obscure a

China	salad	royal
collar	final	spectacles
lizard	climate	crystal
manager	real	several
Cinderella	medal	hospital
umbrella	loyal	emerald

LESSON 274: OBSCURE A – PART 3 (WORD BUILDING)

The instructor:

- Tells children that in the lesson words, *a* sounds like *obscure a* and is pronounced as *uh*.
- Points at the *a*, makes the associated *obscure a* (*uh*) sound, and asks children to repeat the sound.

For each word, the instructor:

- Displays the word, asks children to sound out the word, and allows children to decipher the word with minimal assistance.
- Recites the word aloud and directs children to:
    1. Build the word out of letter tiles.
    2. Point at each letter tile in the word while making the related sound.

obscure a

distant	Scotland	account
instant	Holland	errand
servant	fisherman	balance
giant	German	arrest
currant	disappoint	madam
vacant	appear	allow
arrange	disappear	breakfast
balloon		

LESSON 275: OBSCURE E (WORD BUILDING)

The instructor:

- Tells children that in the lesson words, *e* sounds like *obscure e* and is pronounced as *uh*.
- Points at the *e*, makes the associated *obscure e* (*uh*) sound, and asks children to repeat the sound.

For each word, the instructor:

- Displays the word, asks children to sound out the word, and allows children to decipher the word with minimal assistance.
- Recites the word aloud and directs children to:
  1. Build the word out of letter tiles.
  2. Point at each letter tile in the word while making the related sound.

obscure e

jewel	vessel	present
cruel	gravel	agent
camel	level	silent
angel	travel	absence
barrel	satchel	mitten
towel	bushel	passenger
chisel	moment	children
flannel		

LESSON 276: OBSCURE O – PART 1 (WORD BUILDING)

The instructor:

- Tells children that in the lesson words, *o* sounds like *obscure o* and is pronounced as *uh*.
- Points at the *o*, makes the associated *obscure o* (*uh*) sound, and asks children to repeat the sound.

For each word, the instructor:

- Displays the word, asks children to sound out the word, and allows children to decipher the word with minimal assistance.
- Recites the word aloud and directs children to:
    1. Build the word out of letter tiles.
    2. Point at each letter tile in the word while making the related sound.

obscure o

commence	confess	connect
complete	concern	content
complaint	conclude	contain
welcome	control	console
tiresome	consent	lion
handsome		

LESSON 277: OBSCURE O – PART 2 (WORD BUILDING)

The instructor:

- Tells children that in the lesson words, *o* sounds like *obscure o* and is pronounced as *uh*.
- Points at the *o*, makes the associated *obscure o* (*uh*) sound, and asks children to repeat the sound.

For each word, the instructor:

- Displays the word, asks children to sound out the word, and allows children to decipher the word with minimal assistance.
- Recites the word aloud and directs children to:
  1. Build the word out of letter tiles.
  2. Point at each letter tile in the word while making the related sound.

obscure o

melon	seldom	gallop
lemon	blossoms	occur
lemonade	bottom	offend
ribbon	parrot	conductor
wagon	pilot	hammock
cannon		

LESSON 278: OBSCURE U (WORD BUILDING)

The instructor:

- Tells children that in the lesson words, *u* sounds like *obscure u* and is pronounced as *uh*.
- Points at the *u*, makes the associated *obscure u* (*uh*) sound, and asks children to repeat the sound.

For each word, the instructor:

- Displays the word, asks children to sound out the word, and allows children to decipher the word with minimal assistance.
- Recites the word aloud and directs children to:
  1. Build the word out of letter tiles.
  2. Point at each letter tile in the word while making the related sound.

obscure u

suppose	subtract	album
suggest	circus	syrup
succeed	Saturday	stirrup

LESSON 279: COMBINATION – EN=N (WORD BUILDING)

The instructor:

- Tells children that in the lesson words, *en* sounds like *n*.
- Points at the *en*, makes the associated *n* sound, and asks children to repeat the sound.

For each word, the instructor:

- Displays the word, asks children to sound out the word, and allows children to decipher the word with minimal assistance.
- Recites the word aloud and directs children to:
    1. Build the word out of letter tiles.
    2. Point at each letter tile in the word while making the related sound.

en = n

golden	stolen
open	widen
chosen	kitten
broken	sweeten
frozen	maiden
seven	sudden
given	

LESSON 280: COMBINATION – IN=N (WORD BUILDING)

The instructor:

- Tells children that in the lesson words, *in* sounds like *n*.
- Points at the *in*, makes the associated *n* sound, and asks children to repeat the sound.

For each word, the instructor:

- Displays the word, asks children to sound out the word, and allows children to decipher the word with minimal assistance.
- Recites the word aloud and directs children to:
    1. Build the word out of letter tiles.
    2. Point at each letter tile in the word while making the related sound.

in = n

basin

raisin

LESSON 281: COMBINATION – ON=N (WORD BUILDING)

The instructor:

- Tells children that in the lesson words, *on* sounds like *n*.
- Points at the *on*, makes the associated *n* sound, and asks children to repeat the sound.

For each word, the instructor:

- Displays the word, asks children to sound out the word, and allows children to decipher the word with minimal assistance.
- Recites the word aloud and directs children to:
    1. Build the word out of letter tiles.
    2. Point at each letter tile in the word while making the related sound.

on = n

button   lesson
cotton   poison
season   prison
reason

LESSON 282: COMBINATION – TEN=N (WORD BUILDING)

The instructor:

- Tells children that in the lesson words, *ten* sounds like *n*.
- Points at the *ten*, makes the associated *n* sound, and asks children to repeat the sound.

For each word, the instructor:

- Displays the word, asks children to sound out the word, and allows children to decipher the word with minimal assistance.
- Recites the word aloud and directs children to:
    1. Build the word out of letter tiles.
    2. Point at each letter tile in the word while making the related sound.

ten = n

glisten
often
soften
listen
hasten

ELEMENTARY PHONICS

LESSON 283: COMBINATION – EL=L (WORD BUILDING)

The instructor:

- Tells children that in the lesson words, *el* sounds like *l*.
- Points at the *el*, makes the associated *l* sound, and asks children to repeat the sound.

For each word, the instructor:

- Displays the word, asks children to sound out the word, and allows children to decipher the word with minimal assistance.
- Recites the word aloud and directs children to:
  1. Build the word out of letter tiles.
  2. Point at each letter tile in the word while making the related sound.

el = l

mantel

tassel

shrivel

ravel

LESSON 284: COMBINATION – EX=EGZ (WORD BUILDING)

The instructor:

- Tells children that in the lesson words, *ex* sounds like *egz*.
- Points at the *ex*, makes the associated *egz* sound, and asks children to repeat the sound.

For each word, the instructor:

- Displays the word, asks children to sound out the word, and allows children to decipher the word with minimal assistance.
- Recites the word aloud and directs children to:
    1. Build the word out of letter tiles.
    2. Point at each letter tile in the word while making the related sound.

ex = egz

examine
example
exact
exactly
exist
exert

LESSON 285: MISCELLANEOUS – REVIEW 1 (WORD BUILDING)

For each word, the instructor:

- Displays the word, asks children to sound out the word, and allows children to decipher the word with minimal assistance.

- Recites the word aloud and directs children to:
    1. Build the word out of letter tiles.
    2. Point at each letter tile in the word while making the related sound.

Review

dismiss	inquire	invent
disgust	incline	invite
dislike	impure	interrupt
dispute	include	enclose
display	increase	engage
distress	indeed	enemy
divide	injure	entire
direct	injury	entirely
inside	intend	

LESSON 286: MISCELLANEOUS – REVIEW 2 (WORD BUILDING)

For each word, the instructor:

- Displays the word, asks children to sound out the word, and allows children to decipher the word with minimal assistance.
- Recites the word aloud and directs children to:
  1. Build the word out of letter tiles.
  2. Point at each letter tile in the word while making the related sound.

Review

enter	unknown	excuse
unload	until	explode
unlike	uproar	explain
unwise	upset	extreme
uneasy	excite	express
untwist	excel	expect
unjust	exercise	exchange
untie	except	

LESSON 287: MISCELLANEOUS – REVIEW 3 (WORD BUILDING)

For each word, the instructor:

- Displays the word, asks children to sound out the word, and allows children to decipher the word with minimal assistance.
- Recites the word aloud and directs children to:
    1. Build the word out of letter tiles.
    2. Point at each letter tile in the word while making the related sound.

Review

potato	burrow	dangerous
pocket	sensible	instead
palace	eleven	nobody
shoulder	disease	habit
Japan	animal	robin
Japanese	repair	bridle
parasol	blanket	kitchen
furrow	frolic	

LESSON 288: MISCELLANEOUS – REVIEW 4 (WORD BUILDING)

For each word, the instructor:

- Displays the word, asks children to sound out the word, and allows children to decipher the word with minimal assistance.

- Recites the word aloud and directs children to:
    1. Build the word out of letter tiles.
    2. Point at each letter tile in the word while making the related sound.

Review

complain	certain	carpet
absent	successful	partridge
curtain	market	sharpen
lullaby	discover	alarm
awkward	Monday	undone
possible	depart	cousin
linen	August	Muffet
graceful	because	money
delay		

LESSON 289: MISCELLANEOUS – REVIEW 5 (WORD BUILDING)

For each word, the instructor:

- Displays the word, asks children to sound out the word, and allows children to decipher the word with minimal assistance.
- Recites the word aloud and directs children to:
    1. Build the word out of letter tiles.
    2. Point at each letter tile in the word while making the related sound.

Review

compare	thousands	parents
quarrel	honeycomb	Santa Claus
scarlet	shovel	troublesome
almond	garden	comfortable
prepare	advance	among
uncover	harness	monkey
honey	company	reward

LESSON 290: COMBINATION – PH=F (WORD BUILDING)

The instructor:

- Tells children that in the lesson words, *ph* sounds like *f*.
- Points at the *ph*, makes the associated *f* sound, and asks children to repeat the sound.

For each word, the instructor:

- Displays the word, asks children to sound out the word, and allows children to decipher the word with minimal assistance.
- Recites the word aloud and directs children to:
    1. Build the word out of letter tiles.
    2. Point at each letter tile in the word while making the related sound.

ph = f

Philip	photograph	camphor
Philippine	phonics	nephew
Ralph	Joseph	elephant
telephone	orphan	alphabet
telegraph	Sulphur	geography
pheasant	cipher	

LESSON 291: COMBINATION – GH=F (WORD BUILDING)

The instructor:

- Tells children that in the lesson words, *gh* sounds like *f*.
- Points at the *gh*, makes the associated *f* sound, and asks children to repeat the sound.

For each word, the instructor:

- Displays the word, asks children to sound out the word, and allows children to decipher the word with minimal assistance.
- Recites the word aloud and directs children to:
    1. Build the word out of letter tiles.
    2. Point at each letter tile in the word while making the related sound.

gh = f

cough	roughest	laugh
coughing	tough	laughing
trough	toughen	laughter
rough	enough	

LESSON 292: COMBINATION – MN=M (WORD BUILDING)

The instructor:

- Tells children that in the lesson words, *mn* sounds like *m*.
- Points at the *mn*, makes the associated *m* sound, and asks children to repeat the sound.

For each word, the instructor:

- Displays the word, asks children to sound out the word, and allows children to decipher the word with minimal assistance.
- Recites the word aloud and directs children to:
    1. Build the word out of letter tiles.
    2. Point at each letter tile in the word while making the related sound.

mn = m

hymn   solemn
autumn   condemn
column

LESSON 293: COMBINATION – CH=K (WORD BUILDING)

The instructor:

- Tells children that in the lesson words, *ch* sounds like *k*.
- Points at the *ch*, makes the associated *k* sound, and asks children to repeat the sound.

For each word, the instructor:

- Displays the word, asks children to sound out the word, and allows children to decipher the word with minimal assistance.
- Recites the word aloud and directs children to:
    1. Build the word out of letter tiles.
    2. Point at each letter tile in the word while making the related sound.

ch = k

ache	school	anchor
echo	scholar	orchestra
Christmas	scheme	stomach
chorus	schooner	

LESSON 294: COMBINATION – CH=SH (WORD BUILDING)

The instructor:

- Tells children that in the lesson words, *ch* sounds like *sh*.
- Points at the *ch*, makes the associated *sh* sound, and asks children to repeat the sound.

For each word, the instructor:

- Displays the word, asks children to sound out the word, and allows children to decipher the word with minimal assistance.
- Recites the word aloud and directs children to:
    1. Build the word out of letter tiles.
    2. Point at each letter tile in the word while making the related sound.

ch = sh

Chicago　　Champlain
chute　　　ruching
Charlotte

LESSON 295: COMBINATION – SC=S (WORD BUILDING)

The instructor:

- Tells children that in the lesson words, *sc* sounds like *s*.
- Points at the *sc*, makes the associated *s* sound, and asks children to repeat the sound.

For each word, the instructor:

- Displays the word, asks children to sound out the word, and allows children to decipher the word with minimal assistance.
- Recites the word aloud and directs children to:
    1. Build the word out of letter tiles.
    2. Point at each letter tile in the word while making the related sound.

SC = S

scent   **scissors**

scene   **scythe**

scenery

LESSON 296: COMBINATION – I=Y (WORD BUILDING)

The instructor:

- Tells children that in the lesson words, *i* sounds like *y*.
- Points at the *i*, makes the associated *y* sound, and asks children to repeat the sound.

For each word, the instructor:

- Displays the word, asks children to sound out the word, and allows children to decipher the word with minimal assistance.
- Recites the word aloud and directs children to:
  1. Build the word out of letter tiles.
  2. Point at each letter tile in the word while making the related sound.

i = y

onion
union
million
brilliant
opinion
companion

Italian
Spaniard
Daniel
warrior
familiar

LESSON 297: COMBINATION – I=LONG E (WORD BUILDING)

The instructor:

- Tells children that in the lesson words, *i* sounds like *long e*.
- Points at the *i*, makes the associated *long e* sound, and asks children to repeat the sound.

For each word, the instructor:

- Displays the word, asks children to sound out the word, and allows children to decipher the word with minimal assistance.
- Recites the word aloud and directs children to:
    1. Build the word out of letter tiles.
    2. Point at each letter tile in the word while making the related sound.

i = long e

trio   ravine
marine   police
magazine   valise
machine

LESSON 298: COMBINATION – QU=K (WORD BUILDING)

The instructor:

- Tells children that in the lesson words, *qu* sounds like *k*.
- Points at the *qu*, makes the associated *k* sound, and asks children to repeat the sound.

For each word, the instructor:

- Displays the word, asks children to sound out the word, and allows children to decipher the word with minimal assistance.
- Recites the word aloud and directs children to:
    1. Build the word out of letter tiles.
    2. Point at each letter tile in the word while making the related sound.

qu = k

mosquito

opaque

conquer

lacquer

LESSON 299: COMBINATION – DI=J (WORD BUILDING)

The instructor:

- Tells children that in the lesson words, *di* sounds like *j*.
- Points at the *di*, makes the associated *j* sound, and asks children to repeat the sound.

For each word, the instructor:

- Displays the word, asks children to sound out the word, and allows children to decipher the word with minimal assistance.
- Recites the word aloud and directs children to:
    1. Build the word out of letter tiles.
    2. Point at each letter tile in the word while making the related sound.

di = j

soldier
soldiers
soldierly
soldiering

LESSON 300: COMBINATION – TI=CH (WORD BUILDING)

The instructor:

- Tells children that in the lesson words, *ti* sounds like *ch*.
- Points at the *ti*, makes the associated *ch* sound, and asks children to repeat the sound.

For each word, the instructor:

- Displays the word, asks children to sound out the word, and allows children to decipher the word with minimal assistance.
- Recites the word aloud and directs children to:
    1. Build the word out of letter tiles.
    2. Point at each letter tile in the word while making the related sound.

ti = ch

suggestion
question
digestion
ingestion

LESSON 301: COMBINATION – SILENT H (WORD BUILDING)

The instructor:

- Tells children that in the lesson words, the *h* is silent.
- Points at the *h*, makes no sound, and asks children to repeat the (lack of) sound.

For each word, the instructor:

- Displays the word, asks children to sound out the word, and allows children to decipher the word with minimal assistance.
- Recites the word aloud and directs children to:
    1. Build the word out of letter tiles.
    2. Point at each letter tile in the word while making the related sound.

silent h

exhaust	honor
John	honest
heir	ghost
hour	Rhine

LESSON 302: COMBINATION – ET=LONG A (WORD BUILDING)

The instructor:

- Tells children that in the lesson words, *et* sounds like *long a*.
- Points at the *et*, makes the associated *long a* sound, and asks children to repeat the sound.

For each word, the instructor:

- Displays the word, asks children to sound out the word, and allows children to decipher the word with minimal assistance.
- Recites the word aloud and directs children to:
    1. Build the word out of letter tiles.
    2. Point at each letter tile in the word while making the related sound.

et = long a

bouquet
croquet
sachet
crochet
trebuchet
ricochet

LESSON 303: COMBINATIONS – CE/SI=SH (WORD BUILDING)

The instructor:

- Tells children that in the lesson words, *ce* sounds like *sh*.
- Points at the *ce*, makes the associated *sh* sound, and asks children to repeat the sound.
- Repeats the above steps for *si*.

For each word, the instructor:

- Displays the word, asks children to sound out the word, and allows children to decipher the word with minimal assistance.
- Recites the word aloud and directs children to:
    1. Build the word out of letter tiles.
    2. Point at each letter tile in the word while making the related sound.

ce = sh   si = sh

ocean   excursion

permission

LESSON 304: COMBINATION – CI=SH (WORD BUILDING)

The instructor:

- Tells children that in the lesson words, *ci* sounds like *sh*.
- Points at the *ci*, makes the associated *sh* sound, and asks children to repeat the sound.

For each word, the instructor:

- Displays the word, asks children to sound out the word, and allows children to decipher the word with minimal assistance.
- Recites the word aloud and directs children to:
    1. Build the word out of letter tiles.
    2. Point at each letter tile in the word while making the related sound.

ci = sh

musician
physician
precious
delicious
special

LESSON 305: COMBINATION – TI=SH (WORD BUILDING)

The instructor:

- Tells children that in the lesson words, *ti* sounds like *sh*.
- Points at the *ti*, makes the associated *sh* sound, and asks children to repeat the sound.

For each word, the instructor:

- Displays the word, asks children to sound out the word, and allows children to decipher the word with minimal assistance.
- Recites the word aloud and directs children to:
    1. Build the word out of letter tiles.
    2. Point at each letter tile in the word while making the related sound.

ti = sh

combination	promotion	mention
correction	relation	attention
collection	recitation	intention
objection	invitation	position
action	vacation	condition
station	notion	addition
nation	motion	

LESSON 306: MISCELLANEOUS – REVIEW 1 (WORD BUILDING)

For each word, the instructor:

- Displays the word, asks children to sound out the word, and allows children to decipher the word with minimal assistance.

- Recites the word aloud and directs children to:
    1. Build the word out of letter tiles.
    2. Point at each letter tile in the word while making the related sound.

Review

important	buttercups
snowflakes	powerless
snowbirds	president
forbid	fastest
forsake	today
overload	costliest
postpone	pavement

LESSON 307: MISCELLANEOUS – REVIEW 2 (WORD BUILDING)

For each word, the instructor:

- Displays the word, asks children to sound out the word, and allows children to decipher the word with minimal assistance.
- Recites the word aloud and directs children to:
    1. Build the word out of letter tiles.
    2. Point at each letter tile in the word while making the related sound.

Review

mistake
oatmeal
excitement
snarl
railroad
lonesome
diamonds

postage
gentleman
holiday
subtraction
twilight
tomorrow

LESSON 308: MISCELLANEOUS – REVIEW 3 (WORD BUILDING)

For each word, the instructor:

- Displays the word, asks children to sound out the word, and allows children to decipher the word with minimal assistance.
- Recites the word aloud and directs children to:
  1. Build the word out of letter tiles.
  2. Point at each letter tile in the word while making the related sound.

Review

patient	underneath
mistletoe	messenger
medicine	janitor
fireman	unfold
different	hundred
office	anchor
beneath	

LESSON 309: MISCELLANEOUS – REVIEW 4 (WORD BUILDING)

For each word, the instructor:

- Displays the word, asks children to sound out the word, and allows children to decipher the word with minimal assistance.
- Recites the word aloud and directs children to:
    1. Build the word out of letter tiles.
    2. Point at each letter tile in the word while making the related sound.

Review

druggist electric
valuable probably
yesterday farther
perfect darling
remain forest
direction piano
parade

REFERENCES AND ADDITIONAL READING

1. *Cover Image* (CC0 1.0 Universal Creative Commons Public Domain Dedication)
   a. Source: https://pixabay.com/en/letters-a-abc-alphabet-literacy-67046/
   b. License: https://creativecommons.org/publicdomain/zero/1.0/

2. *Book Adapted from Word Mastery by Florence Akin (1913, {PD-US})*
   a. Online Source: https://archive.org/details/wordmasteryacou00akingoog
   b. License: This work is in the public domain in the United States because it was published (or registered with the U.S. Copyright Office) before January 1, 1923.

3. *Three Little Pigs Story from First Reader by Harriette Taylor Treadwell and Margaret Free (1911, {PD-US})*
   a. Online Source: https://archive.org/details/readlit1stread01free
   b. License: This work is in the public domain in the United States because it was published (or registered with the U.S. Copyright Office) before January 1, 1923.

4. *Three Little Pigs Images by L. Leslie Brooke (1904, {PD-US})*
   a. Sample Online Source: https://en.wikipedia.org/wiki/File:Three_little_pigs_1904_straw_house.jpg
   b. License: This work is in the public domain in the United States because it was published (or registered with the U.S. Copyright Office) before January 1, 1923.

5. *Three Little Pigs Images by Dick Hartley and L. Kirby-Parrish (1914, {PD-US})*
   a. Online Source: https://www.gutenberg.org/files/32504/32504-h/32504-h.htm
   b. License: This work is in the public domain in the United States because it was published (or registered with the U.S. Copyright Office) before January 1, 1923.

6. *Mother Goose Poems from The Real Mother Goose ill by Blanche Fisher Wright (1916, {PD-US})*
   a. Online Source: https://archive.org/details/realmothergoosewrig
   b. License: This work is in the public domain in the United States because it was published (or registered with the U.S. Copyright Office) before January 1, 1923.

7. *All Other Clip Art (CC0 1.0 Universal Creative Commons Public Domain Dedication)*
   a. Source: https://openclipart.org/
   b. License: https://creativecommons.org/publicdomain/zero/1.0/

ABOUT THE AUTHOR

Sonja Glumich is a scientist, educator, wife, and mother who is inspired by Charlotte Mason's living works approach to homeschooling. She is the founder of Under the Home (underthehome.org), an online homeschool curriculum featuring low-cost courses in art history, poetry, prose, music, history, science, studio art, mathematics, reading, and Shakespeare. Sonja and her husband homeschool their three school-aged children using the Under the Home curriculum as featured in this book.

Sonja graduated magna cum laude with bachelor's degrees in biology, chemistry, and computer science and later earned a master's degree in information technology. She has also completed education classes and student teaching leading to certification to teach secondary science.

Sonja has experience teaching children of all ages, from preschool to graduate school, including as a middle school and high school science public school teacher. She has also served as an Adjunct Professor for Syracuse University. She currently works as a computer scientist for the Air Force Research Laboratory. Her current research and education interests are security systems engineering, cyber vulnerability assessments, and everything homeschooling.